LANGUAGE AND LITERACY SERIES

Dorothy S. Strickland, Founding Editor
Celia Genishi and Donna E. Alvermann, Series Editors
ADVISORY BOARD: Richard Allington, Kathryn Au, Bernice Cullinan, Colette Daiute,
Anne Haas Dyson, Carole Edelsky, Mary Juzwik, Susan Lytle, Django Paris, Timothy Shanahan

continued

For volumes in the NCRLL Collection (edited by JoBeth Allen and Donna E. Alvermann) and the Practitioners Bookshelf Series (edited by Celia Genishi and Donna E. Alvermann), as well as other titles in this series, please visit www.tcpress.com.

POSE
WOBBLE
FLOW

A Culturally Proactive Approach to Literacy Instruction

Antero Garcia and
Cindy O'Donnell-Allen

Foreword by Linda Christensen

TEACHERS COLLEGE PRESS
TEACHERS COLLEGE | COLUMBIA UNIVERSITY
NEW YORK AND LONDON

NATIONAL WRITING PROJECT

National Writing Project
Berkeley, CA

Published simultaneously by Teachers College Press, 1234 Amsterdam Avenue, New York, NY 10027 and the National Writing Project, 2105 Bancroft Way, Berkeley, CA 94720-1042.

Through its mission, the National Writing Project (NWP) focuses the knowledge, expertise, and leadership of our nation's educators on sustained efforts to help youth become successful writers and learners. NWP works in partnership with local Writing Project sites, located on nearly 200 university and college campuses, to provide high-quality professional development in schools, universities, libraries, museums, and after-school programs. NWP envisions a future where every person is an accomplished writer, engaged learner, and active participant in a digital, interconnected world.

Library of Congress Cataloging-in-Publication Data

Garcia, Antero.
  Pose, wobble, flow : a culturally proactive approach to literacy instruction /
Antero Garcia, Cindy O'Donnell-Allen ; foreword by Linda Christensen.
      pages cm. — (Language and literacy series)
  Includes bibliographical references and index.
  ISBN 978-0-8077-5652-2 (pbk. : alk. paper)
  ISBN 978-0-8077-5664-5 (hardcover : alk. paper)
  ISBN 978-0-8077-7435-9 (ebook)
     1. Language arts (Secondary) 2. Culturally relevant pedagogy.
  I. O'Donnell-Allen, Cindy. II. Title.
  LB1631.G235 2015
    428.0071'2—dc23   2015019056

ISBN 978-0-8077-5652-2 (paper)
ISBN 978-0-8077-5664-5 (hardcover)
ISBN 978-0-8077-7435-9 (ebook)

Printed on acid-free paper
Manufactured in the United States of America

22 21 20 19 18 17   8 7 6 5 4 3

This book is dedicated to our respective spouses,
Ally and Will,
for their patience during our
many wobbles while producing this work,
and to our National Writing Project colleagues,
who have long understood the
imperative of vulnerable learning

Contents

Foreword

I still recall a day, almost 40 years ago, when I left my classroom in tears. I crossed the hall to see Mrs. Leona Wallace, who was the liaison between the African American community and the school. She was a loving and skilled mentor who taught me about racial politics during my first years of teaching. For example, don't ask students to call you by your first name because their parents taught them that a title and a surname is a mark of respect, one that many of them had been denied.

I was a White girl from a small, White town who landed a job as a temporary Title I Reading teacher at Jefferson High School, located in the heart of a predominantly working-class African American neighborhood in Portland, Oregon. I was sure that I could not return to face my freshmen the next day. Mrs. Wallace dried my tears, gave me a volume of Langston Hughes poetry, and pushed me out the door, assuring me that students forgive our mistakes if they know we care about them. She was right.

At one point in my teaching career, I thought, "I will retire when I have one year where I don't screw up." That year never came. I'm now in my 40th year as an educator, and I'm still teaching and still screwing up. I know now what I didn't know as a novice teacher 40 years ago: Every mistake is a chance to reflect, analyze, and revise. Every mistake—and every success—makes me a better teacher. But I also know that I couldn't have made it without a collective of students, teachers, parents, and community members, like Mrs. Leona Wallace, who encouraged me, nurtured me, challenged me, and taught me. And who pushed me to understand that no matter where we teach or who we teach, we are always teaching about race and class.

In their powerful new book, *Pose, Wobble, Flow,* Antero Garcia and Cindy O'Donnell-Allen provide language arts teachers with both a nurturing and a nudging community, a book version of Mrs. Leona Wallace. Their sage and practical advice will help keep our vision and values intact as we struggle in institutions that may or may not be the citadels of idealism where we imagined ourselves teaching. They remind all of us that teaching is not about following directions: it's about listening to our students and paying attention to the social forces that shape their lives; about learning how to navigate department, school, district, and federal rules to benefit our students by "hacking" the system, so we can keep a job while we continue to honor our core beliefs about education. As the authors note:

> There's no such thing as an apolitical position in teaching. Choosing *not* to disrupt the status quo is itself a political choice. In fact, we see it as a capitulation. In this heavily mandated era when it seems that being posed is the only option, adopting a culturally proactive pose in your teaching is not only a subversive act, . . . but a moral imperative. Yes, educational transformation is a gargantuan task, but making even small moves makes a difference. (p. 30)

And they wisely encourage teachers to join with others in this task—collectives of teachers as well as national organizations, like the National Writing Project and the National Council of Teachers of English—and I would add the Teacher Activist Groups that are rising up around the nation in opposition to top-down corporate school initiatives.

Balancing theory and practice, Garcia and O'Donnell-Allen brace each aspect of the book with examples from their own and other teachers' classroom experiences to demonstrate the ways they navigate systemic injustices, like tracking students of color out of rigorous courses, and the still-too-common traditional canonical expectations. They ask teachers to move learning away from memorization, quizzes, and single-text studies into "the sweet spot where youth interests, peer culture, and academic needs intersect."

At our last Oregon Writing Project class, Emily said, "I don't want the class to end because I want to keep thinking and talking and writing about my teaching. What do I do now?" Other members of the class agreed with Emily. Together they created a series of events where teachers convene to continue the conversation: curriculum meet-ups, where they co-create curriculum on a breaking topic, like the Ferguson and Baltimore uprisings; a hiking and writing day in the Columbia Gorge, where they reflect on a knotty issue, student, or curricular choice in their class; an online collaboration across grade and content areas where they share materials and lessons on social justice issues. As teachers, our education does not end after we receive our degrees; we need to create communities of conscience to keep our curriculum aligned with our ideals. *Pose, Wobble, Flow* should be part of that community—a book we study and return to, a mentor like Mrs. Leona Wallace, when we need to recall that real curriculum ties students' lives, history, and academic disciplines together, that teaching is not about achieving perfection or performing "best practices," it's a lifetime pursuit in the company of students and colleagues.

—Linda Christensen

What It Means to Pose, Wobble, and Flow

In *Bird by Bird: Some Instructions on Writing and Life*, Anne Lamott (1995) suggests that writers should write the books they wish to come upon. The book you're reading came about during a coffee-break conversation we were having one chilly day on the Colorado State University campus where we teach. As we walked back to our university offices from the student union, we discussed some challenges we were both facing in our courses with preservice English Language Arts (ELA) teachers. As soon-to-be teachers, our students were understandably preoccupied with the "how-to" aspects of teaching: writing standards-based lesson plans, designing meaningful projects for their future students, figuring out how to grade them fairly, and so forth. We felt confident that many of the books we had assigned in our current courses would help them with these practical tasks, such as *Teaching for Joy and Justice* (Christensen, 2009), *Teaching English by Design* (Smagorinsky, 2007), and *Supporting Students in a Time of Core Standards* (Wessling, 2011).

Because we were (and are) equally committed to the "why" behind the "how" of pedagogical practices in the English Language Arts classroom, however, we also assigned a parallel set of texts that were primarily theoretical in nature, like Paulo Freire's *Pedagogy of the Oppressed* (1970) and excerpts from bell hooks's *Teaching to Transgress* (1994) and Allan Johnson's *Privilege, Power, and Difference* (2001). Joined by a commitment to critical pedagogy, the authors of these texts advance the idea that teachers have a special responsibility to teach from a social justice perspective, tackling issues of privilege, problems of equity and access, and the possibilities inherent in social and civic action. These texts routinely problematize that alluring notion that there's a set of best-practice teaching methods somewhere out there that are so foolproof they should come with a money-back guarantee. As hooks points out, "engaged pedagogy recognize[s] that strategies must constantly be changed, invented, reconceptualized to address each new teaching experience" (1994, pp. 10–11).

The links between practice and theory in the texts on our syllabus were obvious to us, but often less so to our students, who routinely complained that the latter set was irrelevant; they just wanted to get on with learning *how* to teach. Furthermore, in their minds, teaching seemed like an apolitical enterprise, or one that ought to be if they didn't want to stir up trouble in their future classrooms. Nearing our university offices at the end of our walk, we reluctantly came to the conclusion that our attempts at cobbling together a collection of articles and chapters from various texts to help our students connect the dots between the "how" and the "why" was not only unsuccessful from their standpoint, but from ours as well. In fact, the mere separation of the texts on our syllabus was actually exacerbating the commonly held belief that when it comes to theory and practice, never the twain shall meet. Our coffee break was over, but our conversation wasn't. It still isn't.

Thus, in this book, we invite you to join the conversation as we follow Anne Lamott's advice to write the book that we have wished to come upon as teachers and teacher educators, one that embraces a dual focus on the principles of culturally proactive teaching and the thinking and teaching practices that accompany them. Throughout the book, we address in conceptual *and* practical ways the challenges present in today's teaching contexts. We fully recognize that these challenges may be daunting, especially at the beginning of your teaching career. Yet we encourage you not to shy away from them, but instead to approach them as opportunities to support the capacities of students as they navigate their ways through an ever-changing and connected world. To help you do that, we offer a framework we call Pose, Wobble, Flow, which will prompt you to maintain the continual focus on personal reflexivity and professional growth that is so necessary for acknowledging how privilege and cultural positionality shape one's practice.

THE POSE, WOBBLE, FLOW FRAMEWORK: WHAT IT IS AND HOW TO USE IT

In the early 1990s, educational researcher Mike Rose traveled to classrooms across the United States to learn more about teachers who were making positive changes in students' lives, their schools, and the profession. His resultant book, *Possible Lives,* focused primarily on career teachers, but he also interviewed a handful of preservice teachers. Predictably, these interviews are peppered with the students' questions and apprehensions, as well as an earnest commitment to the profession, despite the fact that they had yet to step into their own classrooms. What is surprising, perhaps, is Rose's discovery that, though the specific questions asked by the preservice and career teachers he interviewed throughout the book varied depending on where they were in their careers, the act of questioning their practice never disappeared.

He concluded that "good teachers, novice and senior, live their classroom lives, maybe out of necessity, in a domain between principle and uncertainty" (1995, p. 283). If experience bears wisdom, then why is this the case? After years in the profession, shouldn't teachers eventually figure out how to get it right? Maybe not. Personally speaking, we know that though our uncertainties and apprehensions differ from those we experienced in our early years of teaching, we have them all the same. What's changed is that we don't view them as liabilities, but as challenges that can further our professional growth. The Pose, Wobble, Flow (P/W/F) framework has helped us conceptualize this mindset.

These three terms function in a metaphorical sense that reflects the practice of yoga. Even as novices, practitioners of yoga assume particular "poses" (e.g., tree, plank, warrior) designed to strengthen their bodies, lengthen muscles, improve balance, and increase mindfulness through focused breathing and concentration. To progress in yoga, practitioners learn to hold familiar poses for extended periods of time and to gradually add more difficult poses to their repertoire. In so doing, they experience "wobble" as a guaranteed and necessary part of the growth process. While wobble may initially cause frustration, it also signals a commitment to increased discipline and deepened practice. Persisting through wobble produces a satisfying sense of being "in the flow," of focusing oneself so intently on the activity of the moment that time seems to disappear. Flow is also an overall aspect of styles of yoga in a different sense. For example, in *vinyasa flow yoga*, practitioners combine varied poses in a sequence (e.g., sun salutation), attempting to achieve a graceful flow of movement in the process. Repeated P/W/F cycles with new poses are necessary to improve one's strength, balance, and concentration; yoga is a lifelong practice, and one never quite arrives at a perpetual state of flow.

To extend the metaphor to teaching: Like yoga practitioners, teachers who are committed to professional growth also take up stances (or poses) toward their practice, and reflect on areas in which they wobble with the intent of attaining flow—those provisional moments that mark progress in their teaching. In the sections that follow, we unpack the meaning of each of these terms one at a time, show how they work together by drawing on classroom examples, and then make suggestions for steps you can take to enact P/W/F cycles in your own teaching. Before we do that, though, we want to point out three essential features of the model.

First of all, it is framed by a focus on educational equity. Throughout this book, the poses we highlight are centered on re-evaluating the educational needs of *all* students in order to challenge assumptions of equality in pedagogical design and educational reform. Secondly, the P/W/F cycle is not purely linear. If you've observed or been taught by effective teachers, it may seem that they have discovered some hidden answer key containing surefire teaching strategies, engaging assignments, and methods for effortless classroom management. Looking something like Figure I.1, their expertise appears to elevate in a steady line because they know how to move directly from pose to flow.

Figure I.1. Linear Model of Developing Expertise in Experienced Teachers' Practice

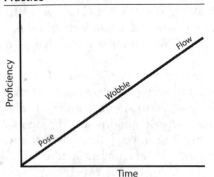

Figure I.2. P/W/F Model of Developing Expertise in Experienced Teachers' Practice

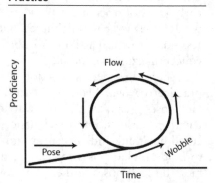

Figure I.3. Recursive Model of Developing Expertise Through Repeated P/W/F Cycles

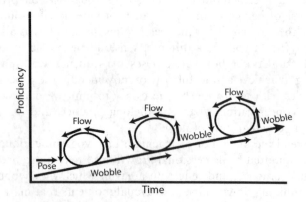

But we can say from experience that even teachers whose practice is apparently seamless to the outside eye will continue to wobble in response to changes in their teaching contexts. Working through these wobbles continuously is an integral part of their commitment to deepened practice. In reality, then, their development looks more like Figure I.2.

As a more accurate reflection of professional growth, the P/W/F model is *not* about an endpoint; it is a framework to help acknowledge how one's practice changes over time and requires constant adaptation. It provides language for the often frustrating feelings of uncertainty inherent in the recursive process of improving one's practice. It also reflects the reality that in teaching, just as in yoga, repeated P/W/F cycles are necessary for continual professional growth (see Figure I.3).

Finally, even though the model as we've described it above often sounds individualistic, we don't intend for it to be. In fact, especially when taking on what we'll describe below as "proactive" poses, we have found that we go through P/W/F cycles most successfully when we collaborate with colleagues who provide moral support and at the same time challenge our thinking.

What Does It Mean to Pose?

There's more to yoga than walking into an exercise studio, unrolling a mat, stretching your muscles, and balancing on one foot. Rather, yoga practitioners deliberately position their bodies in particular ways called *asanas*. The literal translation of *asana* is "seat," conveying an image of stability that enhances meditation. A yoga practitioner often pauses to focus her attention as she moves into a pose, deliberately setting her body in place. She sustains a pose in order to stretch a certain set of muscles and to simultaneously assume a particular mindset. Similarly, our use of the term *pose* in reference to teaching is meant to convey intentionality. A pose is *a stance or mindset you willingly take on as a teacher for well-considered reasons.* In this book, we recommend several poses that you can take up as a teacher, for instance taking a culturally proactive stance toward your practice and seeing yourself as a writer, a curator of curriculum, and so on.

Although the word *pose* often has a pejorative connotation (i.e., one poses in an attempt to trick, dissemble, or cloak true intentions), a more neutral definition also exists. According to the Merriam-Webster Dictionary, to pose can also mean "to assume a posture or attitude, usually for artistic purposes." Etymologically speaking, this form of the word comes from the Late Latin *pausare*, meaning "to stop or rest," and thus is actually a closer cousin to the word *pause*. The word also conveys deliberation. To pose is to "set forth or offer for attention or consideration" (i.e., to pose a question) or to "put or set in place" (i.e., to pose a model). These definitions illuminate that in both yoga and the P/W/F model, the word pose conveys the dimensions of mindfulness suggested by the Latin root *pausare*.

We want to be clear that a pose is far more than a "best practice," which, as we pointed out earlier, is an idea that relies on the myth that some teaching techniques are so foolproof they will work with all students in all contexts for all time. Rather, adopting a pose requires considerable mindfulness, for poses focus on the "why of teaching: why teaching methods work in particular ways in particular settings" (Smagorinsky, 2009, p. 19). As such, they function as touchstones to guide our teaching.

What Does It Mean to Wobble?

The poses you take up in your career will have profound implications for the kind of teacher you intend to be and the impact you and your students will make on the world. The commitment it will take to sustain them will often lead you to wobble. Bob Fecho (2011) defines *wobble* as a naturally occurring circumstance that is not just limited to teaching and learning, but is part of everyday life. He explains that wobble is a calling to attention, a provocation of response. When something wobbles—a wheel on a car, a glass of wine on a waiter's tray, a child's top, the Earth on its axis—we notice. It causes us to stare and consider. Wobble taps us on the shoulder and induces us to ask why. It nudges us toward action. It suggests we get out of our chair and do something. (p. 53)

Wobble occurs routinely in the classroom when something unexpected emerges, such as an unpredictable question that neither the students (nor you, for that matter) can adequately address, or a spat that breaks out between students that has absolutely nothing to do with the academic subject at hand. When wobble occurs, you may feel as if nothing in your teacher education program has prepared you for this, and you may very well be right. Because teaching and learning are complex and alinear processes, because the classroom is a dynamic context, and because students can be mercurial, wobble is guaranteed. In fact, "the messy realities of teaching do not lend themselves simply to the selection and implementation of curricula and methods produced by experts from afar. Ambiguities, uncertainties, and unpredictably [sic] are the substance of teaching" (Cochran-Smith & Lytle, 2009, p. 74). Recognizing that this unpredictability is inherent in teaching can make wobble easier to deal with over time, depending on one's degree of comfort with ambiguity.

To return to the yoga metaphor for a moment, experienced practitioners not only expect to wobble, they welcome it:

When holding a yoga posture, you want to go to your edge. The edge is a place where you feel a deep stretch in your body or you feel the body working hard, but not going past that to where you hurt yourself or overwork the body. . . . try to relax into the edge by consciously relaxing the muscles that are stretching and the muscles that do not need to work in the pose. (Burgin, 2012, "Asanas: Yoga Postures" section, para. 3)

Likewise, in teaching, it's essential to remember that although you and your students may not feel comfortable when you wobble, this discomfort is natural because you are "going to your edge."

Fecho (2011) explains that "wobble . . . marks a liminal state, a state of transition. Where there is wobble, change is occurring. . . . That which was once *this* is moving slowly—at least at first—toward becoming *that*" (p. 53). As he points out, because wobble introduces instability into our lives, our instincts may be to avoid it at all costs, or when it does occur, to attempt to restore order, but we also have another option: We can choose to "construct meaning from an experience different from what might have been imagined" before (p. 54). In other words, when you wobble, it doesn't mean that you're failing. Rather, it signals that you are pursuing worthwhile poses that require learning, reflection, and professional growth. As Cindy reminds her students, "You gotta wobble if you ever want to flow."

What Is Flow?

Wobbling sometimes entails considerable effort and resolve that can achieve worthwhile results, yet it's not a state you can maintain inevitably. The good news is that "flow," the final stage of P/W/F, is achievable. Otherwise, we ourselves most likely would have left the profession long ago. As the preeminent scholar on *flow*, Mihaly Csikszentmihalyi (2008) defines it as a "sense of exhilaration, a deep sense of enjoyment that is long cherished and becomes a landmark in memory for what life should be like" (p. 3). This "harmonious, effortless" state (p. 40) occurs when we feel immersed in achieving a worthwhile goal that is precisely appropriate for our level of ability. That is, the goal-oriented activity we are engaged in is just difficult enough that we feel challenged rather than overwhelmed, yet not so easy to reach that we feel bored. Flow experiences are so intense that we lose track of time and temporarily escape other everyday concerns. We want to feel the joy and fulfillment they induce again and again; thus, over time, flow experiences "add up to a sense of mastery—or perhaps better, a sense of *participation* in determining the content of life" (p. 4). Ultimately, "this is the way the self grows" (p. 42) because individuals become more capable and skilled as a result of the flow experience.

It's worth noting that although Csikszentmihalyi's work on flow is primarily associated with a psychological state as it is experienced in particular moments in time, he also makes reference to the connections between flow and yoga, explaining that "[the] similarities between Yoga and flow are extremely strong; in fact it makes sense to think of Yoga as a very thoroughly planned flow activity" (p. 105). He goes on to say that "[it] is not unreasonable to regard Yoga as one of the oldest and most systematic methods of producing the flow experience" (p. 106). As alluded to in our overview of the P/W/F model above, we are likewise using the term flow in a dual sense to refer to both the moments of psychological well-being one experiences in singular moments during the everyday course of teaching, and the larger overall project of linking complementary poses together over the span of one's teaching career.

Csikszentmihalyi points out that the approach one takes to achieving flow depends on the activity in which one is engaged. That's because both the goals and the feedback inherent in particular activities vary in specificity. For instance, in activities like rock climbing, the goal is concrete, and the feedback is clear and immediate; if you are pursuing a peak, you'll know when you've reached it. Other more open-ended activities have more ambiguous goals and outcomes, however. Csikszentmihalyi offers writing music and painting pictures as examples. Both songwriters and painters who sit down in front of a blank canvas or page (or screen) may have a vague concept toward which they are working, but as the art emerges, they may make countless adjustments and new decisions that result in a product they probably didn't imagine from the start. Csikszentmihalyi advises that in "activities, where goals are not clearly set in advance, a person must develop a strong personal sense of what she intends to do. . . . Without such internal guidelines, it is impossible to experience flow" (p. 56).

We believe teaching falls into the latter open-ended category. Like painters attempting to produce a work of art, as teachers, our ultimate goal is to support students' learning, but our attempts to do so vary according to the specific challenges presented in the circumstances and context at hand. For instance, when students' learning needs differ across a particular class, it can be difficult to find one teaching approach that will accommodate and engage all of them. Thus the goals for both painters and teachers are sufficiently vague as to make it difficult to know whether or not we are succeeding on a moment-by-moment basis. This is why poses are so important. As we said before, they function as touchstones to guide our teaching. Reflecting back to our poses during moments of wobble allows us to gauge the progress we and our students are making toward the flow state that will ultimately result in growth. Just as Csikszentmihalyi notes, in our experiences of persisting through wobble to the other side of the flow activity, our identities emerge as more complex, and we feel capable of meeting new challenges as they arise.

As we mentioned previously, however, we don't mean to suggest that movement through the P/W/F cycle is linear and upward in nature. That's just not how teaching works. Remember those changing contexts? They inevitably make us wobble anew and necessarily require that we shift and refine our poses in response. Yet, just as yoga practitioners flow from pose to pose in a yoga session, each P/W/F cycle builds on the next. In the process, our teaching deepens and our courage to seek out more complex challenges grows as well.

In the sections that follow, we provide two examples to help you see what a P/W/F cycle looks like from start to finish. The first hypothetical example shows how flow might be achieved in response to a challenge presented in a singular instance of wobbling. The second example, from Antero's teaching, demonstrates how he achieved flow in relation to an overarching pose that has framed his career as a culturally proactive teacher—by challenging inequities in the education system that inhibit students' life chances for success within and beyond school.

MOVING FROM POSE TO WOBBLE TO FLOW:
TWO EXAMPLES OF A P/W/F CYCLE

Practitioners of yoga often speak of mindfulness when referring to the meditative aspects of yoga. Even when poses are so challenging that they seem almost impossible to maintain, the experienced practitioner notices what is happening in the moment, observes the sensations his body is experiencing, returns attention to his breathing, and (when in a yoga class with others) relies on the teacher to guide him into the next pose. Over time, yoga practitioners report that these same mindfulness skills can extend beyond the yoga studio into one's reactions to the challenges of everyday life.

Similarly, when dealing with wobble in teaching, remember that reacting is not the same as being reactionary. The former word carries a connotation of reflectiveness and intentionality; the latter implies a knee-jerk, conditioned response. It's helpful to recall that the Latin root for "pose" is *pausare*. Reacting to wobble requires you to pause, observe, and critically read the demands of the context, unpack the assumptions embedded within those demands, and determine mindfully how to respond.

Often, as teachers, we wobble as we decide when to follow mandates that don't sit with us too well. Admittedly, our first impulses are often reactionary, leading us to rant to anyone within earshot about the injustice of "it" all, whatever "it" may be. Sometimes blowing off steam like this is enough and we determine that we can "go along to get along" because in the long run, complying with the mandate will have a pretty inconsequential impact on our teaching and our students' learning. At other times, our wobbling just won't go away. In those circumstances, we can use two strategies to work toward flow:

1. We can work *within* the system by meeting the mandate, but doing so on our terms.
2. We can "work" the system by being subversive.

Again, determining which option to take in a moment of wobble requires that we use our poses as touchstones so that we can react reflectively rather than be reactionary.

Working Within the System

Sometimes you will be asked to comply with routine systemic constraints that conflict with the poses you've adopted as a teacher. Again, in such circumstances we recommend that you pause and critically read the system, then determine how to intentionally proceed in ways that won't require you to compromise your principles. You can often meet the letter of the law while transcending the spirit of the law; that is, you can work within the system, albeit in unexpected ways.

For instance, let's say that you are teaching an 11th-grade English course on American Literature, and the department curriculum requires that you teach *The Crucible* and give a summative assessment to gauge your students' understanding of the play. You have adopted the pose of teaching in ways that make it possible for your students to construct their own knowledge around a particular topic. This commitment implies that your assessment methods will reflect a value for open-ended, inquiry-oriented opportunities for students to express what they have learned. As required, you assign *The Crucible*, but you decide to use the play as the anchor text in a unit focused on the question of what it means to be an American. You select a range of print-based and multimedia texts related to the unit theme written by diverse authors over time, moving beyond the canon to include texts like Martin Luther King's "Letter from a Birmingham Jail," the music video "Fight the Power" by Public Enemy, and *Guilty by Suspicion*, a film by Irwin Winkler about a filmmaker consigned to the Hollywood blacklist.

As you consider a summative assessment for the unit, one of your colleagues reminds you that most of the teachers in your department use an exam on *The Crucible* provided in the resources that accompany the required literature textbook. When you take a look, you find a traditional multiple-choice exam on *The Crucible* with items like this hypothetical one:

> What is the name of the servant who was fired from John and Elizabeth Proctor's household?
>
> A. Rebecca Nurse
> B. Mary Warren
> C. Ruth Putnam
> D. Abigail Williams

The prospect of a ready-made, easily graded test sounds tempting, but on further reflection, you realize that even though answering multiple-choice questions correctly might prove that students had read the play, doing so would require them only to memorize and recall facts. Moreover, giving an objective exam only on *The Crucible* would deny students opportunities to explore the rich array of texts they had read in relation to the unit theme on American identity. Using this test as your final assessment would thus run counter to your constructivist pose for teaching and assessment.

Asking students to create a final project in response to the following prompt, however, would allow them to further develop their thinking:

> What does it mean to be an American? Design a project that draws on *The Crucible*, at least four other texts we have read in this unit, and an experience from your own life to demonstrate your consideration of this question. You can choose the form your project will take, but it should incorporate words, audio, and/or images and should inspire your audience to problematize traditional conceptions of American identity. You can work by yourself or in a small group.

To do well on this project, students would still need to incorporate details from the unit texts, but would also need to synthesize those details with elements of their own experiences in order to create a personally meaningful artifact that addresses a question with no definitive answer. Unlike a multiple-choice test, this final assessment comes with no answer key. Rather, students have considerable freedom to determine the content and form of their project and to work with others or by themselves. This project is thus consistent with the teaching pose described above because it implicitly conveys to students that knowledge is not fixed, but continually developing, and that they are capable of making decisions about their own learning.

The two assessment options also reflect very different views of how you see yourself as a teacher. The multiple-choice test relies on a nameless test-maker who is far removed from your classroom to determine the most important facts students should know about *The Crucible*. The project on American identity, on the other hand, requires you to understand and value your individual students' perspectives. By assigning this project, you've technically worked within the system. You have still met your department's requirement to give a summative assessment over *The Crucible,* a required text in the curriculum. But you haven't compromised your pose about what constitutes meaningful learning for your students because you've viewed assessment as an opportunity for them to construct their own knowledge. By using an active pose as a touchstone, you've maintained your agency as a "deliberative intellectual" (Cochran-Smith & Lytle, 2009) capable of posing yourself rather than being posed in the expected ways implicit in a particular constraint within your teaching context.

Working the System

In some cases like the one above, it's possible to work within the system and simultaneously maintain your commitment to a given pose. Some instances, however, call for the more radical approach of "working the system" instead. Especially early in your career, when you choose to react to wobble by working the system, it's essential that you have a very firm rationale that is grounded in theory, research, and/or the recommendations of professional organizations, so that you can justify what you're doing and why to those in positions of power over you.

A few years into his teaching career, Antero wobbled around the persistent tracking occurring at his school, which ran counter to an overarching pose that guides his practice as a culturally proactive teacher: He was determined to critique and push back against inequitable schooling practices that compromise marginalized students' access to meaningful learning opportunities and life chances within and beyond school.

Antero and his high school students were part of a "small learning community" (SLC), a school-within-a-school cluster of students with the same group of teachers. The community included the majority of the English language learners (ELLs) at the school. While another SLC offered honors and AP classes, the students in Antero's SLC were not afforded these options. After becoming aware of advocacy efforts used by the College Board at the time to ensure equal access for all students to AP classes, Antero determined to work the system. He urged his 11th-grade students (who were also all of the 11th-grade students in the SLC) to go to their counselor and demand to be placed in AP courses. When the administration insisted that the demand was too great for one teacher, Antero volunteered to go through the AP training. He also got permission to provide instructional continuity for his students by "looping" the class the subsequent year. This meant that his AP classes included many seniors whom he had taught the previous year. He was thus able to teach his current juniors for two years in a row—once during their junior year and then again during their senior year when a new group of 11th-graders was encouraged to advocate for participation in AP classes in their senior year.

Though Antero's students did not pass the AP exam during the first year of the experiment, passing a test wasn't the point of this work. What mattered most was that students *acted like* and *perceived themselves to be* AP students. Even though prior to this experience, the unspoken caste system of urban schooling had labeled them as the ELL students who would pull down the school's already dismal test scores each year, these students proved themselves able to tackle complicated texts by authors like Faulkner, Woolf, Morrison, and Ellison. They rose to the higher expectations of an AP course and incidentally showed more significant gains in their ELA growth than any of the seniors Antero had taught previously.

Antero's response to a tracking policy that caused him to wobble by challenging his overarching pose of culturally proactive teaching embodies the advice we gave earlier in this chapter. Rather than being reactionary, Antero stepped back and critically read the inequitable assumptions embedded in his teaching context, which reinforced his conviction that the circumstances were unacceptable. Then, he and his students dismantled the seemingly insurmountable obstacles in their path toward educational equity and access. Antero justified his position with reference to a reputable organization, the College Board. He gave his students their marching orders, which they gladly followed, becoming advocates for their own educational rights in the process. In response to administrative pushback, he proved his willingness to follow through by volunteering for additional AP training and looping with his students the following year. Antero and his students experienced flow by collectively raising their voices to enact transgressive change in a tracked educational system that propagated inequitable conditions for learning.

LOOKING AHEAD

As you will see in Chapter 1, the above example from Antero's teaching reflects the overarching pose of being a culturally proactive teacher over the span of one's career. It ties together the following poses in subsequent chapters that we see as central to this overarching commitment:

- *Teacher as Hacker:* This pose in Chapter 2 focuses on creating and sustaining a dialogic curriculum.

- ***Literacy for Civic Engagement:*** This pose in Chapter 3 focuses on supporting the development of students' civic identity.
- ***Teacher as Writer:*** This pose in Chapter 4 focuses on developing an identity as a writer who teaches and a teacher who writes.
- ***Teacher as Curator:*** This pose in Chapter 5 focuses on increasing powerful, culturally proactive reading choices.
- ***Teacher as Designer:*** This pose in Chapter 6 focuses on creating equitable learning environments.

Each chapter reflects the P/W/F model. We offer a specific pose at the start of each chapter, provide tools for working through wobble (e.g., thinking strategies, standards, teaching methods), and use a balance of theory and research, classroom examples, and personal experiences to demonstrate how teachers and students in particular contexts have worked toward achieving flow in relation to the pose. Each chapter concludes with a set of "Provocations" and a list of "Connections"—thinking prompts and digital and print resources designed to extend your consideration as a beginning teacher of the themes and issues presented in the chapter.

In the Conclusion we review major themes and make the case for studying the impact that maintaining a lifelong commitment to culturally proactive teaching has on student learning. Finally, at the end of the book we offer two Appendixes rooted in the P/W/F model. Appendix A provides a step-by-step guide to support you in taking up a critical inquiry stance with other colleagues that is based on thorny issues present in your particular teaching context. Appendix B recaps the poses listed above. Depending on the stage of your career, these resources can be used to guide in-class activities in education courses or as a tool for self-sponsored or site-embedded professional development, especially during your first few years of teaching. Appendix C is a template for developing your own poses and supporting the nuanced directions that your classroom will push you toward. Based on the P/W/F framework, this worksheet should allow you to identify additional culturally proactive teaching practices related to areas of your instruction and career that we have not addressed explicitly in this book. You'll also find a free downloadable and printable version of Appendix C online at the Teachers College Press website (teacherscollegepress.com/).

As a final note, we want to emphasize that the order in which we present the above poses isn't meant to be chronological; nor are the poses themselves meant to be viewed as endpoints you will finally achieve and then—presto!—arrive at teaching perfection. In your work to be a culturally proactive teacher, you're never "finished" with these poses. You'll always experience moments of wobble and continue to grow. Learning entails cognitive movement and is therefore often messy, but also dynamic and real. These poses, then, are touchstones that you will continue to return to in building a lasting and fulfilling career that, to paraphrase Freire (2004), doesn't simply adapt to the world, but transforms it (p. 7).

PROVOCATIONS

1. Keep a journal or diary (digital or nondigital) and begin listing the areas of your practice that you continue to struggle with. Prioritize those areas that require the most in-depth scrutiny. Can you name these as poses? Begin filling out your own pose using the template from Appendix C.

2. Try jotting brief notes in your daily lesson plans or recording a few words on sticky notes that will later jog your memory about classroom events related to your wobble. If it's easier, you can even record voice memos on your phone or computer and listen to them on your way home to reflect on how your teaching went that day. As you interrogate your wobble by inquiring into your practice, what insights are you finding? Where are you experiencing flow?

3. Use the same process above to reflect on your students' work. Seeing this as data for meaningfully informed wobbling, what are your students producing, and what does their work say about your classroom's culture, your teaching practice, your understanding of who your students are? Don't forget that your students are the best source of information about their own learning. Talk to them and try to find common ground.

4. Seek out allies and mentors in your school or district with whom you can share moments of wobble and celebrate moments of flow. Find contexts where you can interact with others to learn more and share what you've learned, such as conferences and professional networks. Stay current in the profession by reading journals and connecting with experienced teachers in online settings.

CONNECTIONS

Explore the following resources for further insight into Pose, Wobble, Flow:

Fecho, Bob. (2011). *Teaching for the Students: Habits of Heart, Mind, and Practice in the Engaged Classroom.*

> Fecho's book has helped provide a foundational understanding around the concept of "wobble," and continues to remind us to put student needs at the forefront of our teaching decisions.

Goldstein, Dana. (2014). *The Teacher Wars.*

> This historical account of U.S. education is a compelling look at the cycles of policy and reform that have shaped the teaching profession. As teachers today wobble with high-stakes testing and shifting definitions of the profession, Goldstein's book offers critical perspective on how these changes have played out in the past.

Singer, Jessica. (2006). *Stirring Up Justice: Writing and Reading to Change the World.*

> Books like Singer's take you into the classrooms of teachers today. She offers illustrations of wobble and moments of flow that all tie to student growth and remind readers of the nuanced differences of our own classrooms.

Educators' Blogs:

> We find it helpful to regularly read from colleagues who wobble publicly in online spaces (a process we expect our students to do— see Chapter 5). Some teacher blogs you might begin with include budtheteacher.com, thejosevilson.com, and dogtrax.edublogs.org.

Books on yoga include:

Burgin, Timothy. (2012). *Yoga for Beginners: A Quick-Start Guide to Practicing Yoga for New Students.*

White, Ganga. (2007). *Yoga Beyond Belief: Insights to Awaken and Deepen Your Practice.*

> These books provide an accessible introduction to the foundations and philosophy of yoga, terminology, tips and instructions, and photographs of basic yoga poses.

CHAPTER 1

Leaning Toward Praxis

What It Means to Be a Culturally Proactive Teacher

In his book *Why School?*, Mike Rose points out that our culture needs "an expanded vocabulary, adequate to both the daily joy and the daily sorrow of our public schools," one that invites "capacious critique" of public education by "[encouraging] both dissent and invention, anger and hope" (2009, p. 152). We have found that the vocabulary of *Pose, Wobble, Flow* we explored in the previous chapter heeds Rose's call, especially when considered in tandem with an overarching pose we refer to as *culturally proactive teaching* that unites all the other poses we will explore in subsequent chapters of the book. Together, the concepts of Pose, Wobble, Flow and culturally proactive teaching form a robust framework that helps us as teachers lean toward *praxis*: that inextricable union between critical reflection on oppressive conditions and the social action necessary to transform the world into a more just and equitable place (see Freire, 1970).

Engaging in culturally proactive praxis requires teachers to critique the "fallacy of cultural neutrality and the homogeneity syndrome in teaching and learning," especially for historically marginalized students (Gay, 2010). We share Geneva Gay's advocacy for "instructional reforms . . . that are grounded in positive beliefs about the cultural heritages and academic potentialities of these students" (p. 23). At the same time, we acknowledge that grappling with issues of race, class, gender, and sexuality while simultaneously striving to teach literacy effectively can be uncomfortable and difficult, thus causing a significant degree of wobble. To be culturally proactive teachers, however, maintaining this dual focus is necessary.

In this chapter, we flesh out the pose of *culturally proactive teaching* by describing how it extends existing theory and by demonstrating how you can use the pose to confront the challenges that teachers face in today's taxing education environment. But first, here are the central elements of this pose:

CULTURALLY PROACTIVE TEACHING:
DEVELOP AN IDENTITY AS A CULTURALLY PROACTIVE TEACHER BY:

> ➤ framing your teaching around a commitment to praxis and questioning existing inequities in schooling and society;

> ➤ anticipating students' needs within your classroom and adjusting your practice to their interests, developing identities, and cultural expertise;

> ➤ articulating your own cultural positionality and reflecting on the ways it shapes your teaching and your students' learning;

> ➤ using the cultural and linguistic backgrounds of your students as resources for their learning; and

> ➤ teaching critical literacy skills that will help your students understand, critique, and contest systemic inequities and take social action to change them.

THEORETICAL BACKGROUND

In creating the term *culturally proactive teaching,* we mean to echo the powerful, existing theories on culturally responsive and culturally sustaining education reviewed below, but also to extend these theories in ways that have been helpful to our thinking and our practice and that we hope will be useful to yours as well. Geneva Gay (2010) defines *culturally responsive teaching* as teaching that uses "the cultural knowledge, prior experiences, frames of reference, and performance styles of ethnically diverse students to make learning encounters more relevant to and effective for them" (p. 29). For more than fifteen years, Gay's pivotal work has challenged educators to confront the disconnect between youth identities and traditional content and styles of teaching in classrooms. In particular, she insists that "teacher preparation programs must be as culturally responsive to ethnic diversity as K–12 classroom instruction" (p. 114). Since then, literacy educators have taken up Gay's charge to teach more responsively, for instance by teaching more texts by diverse authors and by bringing popular youth culture such as movies, comics, technology, and music into the classroom (e.g., Golden, 2001; Herrington, Hodgson, & Moran, 2009; Morrell, 2004; Watkins, 2009).

More recently, researchers Django Paris and H. Samy Alim (2014) have pushed for a framework around "culturally sustaining pedagogy" (see also Paris, 2012). This model looks at the "overdeterministic" (p. 88) links between race, cultural practice, and literacy typically found in culturally relevant frameworks for classroom instruction. In doing so, Paris and Alim advocate for "supporting multilingualism and multiculturalism in practice and perspective for students and teachers" (p. 88) and acknowledging that young people "are enacting race, ethnicity, language, literacy, and cultural practices in both traditional and evolving ways" (p. 90). Pairing this recognition with an acknowledgment of the need for critical reflexivity, they update limited applications of cultural relevancy and push toward a pluralistic, 360-degree perspective of students in schools.

By using the word "proactive," we mean to build respectfully on the work that has gone before us and to acknowledge its impact on our own teaching practices in both secondary and university settings. At the same time, however, we contend that teaching must be more than responsive if we are to address the amalgam of 21st-century demands that teachers face in working with a growing culturally and linguistically diverse student population. Instead, we must *anticipate* students' needs in the context of these demands and adjust our practice both preemptively and in the daily process of working with students in our classrooms. Teasing out the nuances of the word *proactive* has clarified our thinking in this regard because it underscores that teaching requires:

- an ongoing vigilance—before we even step into our classrooms, during the midst of our daily interactions with students, and afterwards, in the quieter moments of reflection on our practice;
- a sense of intentionality and urgency given the unjust world we all inhabit; and, finally,
- an awareness that we *initiate* this work rather than waiting for others to tell us it should be done.

These nuances should make it clear that adopting a pose of culturally proactive teaching requires humility and an innate willingness to accept *wobbling* as we describe it in this book. By its very nature, this pose implies that we will not enter the classroom as all-knowing experts, but as learners with and from our students, their families, and their communities. The ongoing process of understanding how classroom cultures emerge from students' lived experiences is challenging. It requires constant and unyielding attention.

Thus, rather than simply advocating for pedagogy that is "tolerant," a word that sometimes connotes begrudging acknowledgment or even indifference, you can push toward being proactive and anticipatory in your work. This means using what you learn from students and their school community to inform what you do. And while definitions of "culture" encompass more than classifications of race, class, and gender, the persistent and garroting nature of unspoken discriminatory practices in the U.S. dictate that this is one of the most important reasons for adopting a culturally proactive pose in your teaching.

You will wobble around this pose in your classroom, and it is perhaps the most difficult yet generative puzzle that you will never fully solve. Yet working toward flow is particularly important because issues of race, class, and gender are ever-present. They don't disappear into the hallway when we shut the classroom door. Rather, they drench the personal histories and identities both we and our students carry, and they imbue every moment-to-moment transaction that occurs in our classrooms. In reflecting on his own classroom practice, Knaus (2011) writes:

> caring, responsive curriculum and teaching approaches are still limited by my own capacity to reflect on and address race, gender, and class-based privileges that shape everything I do within (and outside of) a classroom (hooks, 1994). This is particularly important as a straight White man; I cannot know what life is like as a young person of color, as a queer youth, or even growing up poor in today's world, but I can learn as much as I can, and develop a team to support me. (p. 89)

Knaus's comments make clear that in addition to learning about the experiences of your students, interrogating your own positionality is imperative. Doing this work is especially important if you are working with historically marginalized students. However, even if you work with a more racially homogeneous and/or affluent group of students, you're not "off the hook" (Johnson, 2001, p. 117). Although you and your students may not experience oppressive conditions directly or on a repeated basis, oppression is inherent in our culture. We contend that if you stay silent, you are endorsing/reinforcing these conditions and perpetuating the cycle of violence (actual and metaphorical) in the lives of others who may not share your privilege. Recognizing that you possess privilege is the first step in using your unearned power for good. Everyone is part of the system, and we all have to push back against it if we are going to transform it.

Here again, we echo the work of Knaus:

> It was (and is) educator responsibility to learn how to prepare White students so that we do not replicate racism, so that we use the ways we are oppressed to help us understand other forms of oppression. If educators do not know how to do this, then it is their responsibility to learn how. This is what it means to be an educator; we have to learn what our students need to learn. (p. 40)

Culturally proactive pedagogy looks critically at how to better meet the needs of *all* the students in our ELA classrooms, whether they are historically marginalized or historically privileged.

WHY BEING A CULTURALLY PROACTIVE TEACHER IS NON-NEGOTIABLE IN TODAY'S WORLD

Adopting this pose and working through the wobble that surrounds it is hard, but it is worthwhile work. An unswerving commitment to it can center your practice in ways that matter to you, to your students, and to all of us. Personally, we've discovered that the pose lends purpose and urgency to our practice—and complicates it—in equal parts, especially in light of the current demands we face in education and in the culture at large.

Historically speaking, it's true that schooling has always been a challenging business. Although the lingo has changed, arguments about the goals of education and about accountability measures to determine whether or not students are meeting them are nothing new. In fact, in 1924, English professor Charles Sutphin Pendleton self-published *The Social Objectives of School English*. There were 1,581 of them! Benjamin Bloom and his colleagues published the *Taxonomy of Educational Objectives* in 1956, which is now commonly referred to as "Bloom's Taxonomy" and which made a big comeback in revised form in 2000 (Anderson, Krathwohl, et al.). (For "A Brief History of Educational Objectives," see Carmen, 2002.) In the mid-1990s, "outcomes" was the term du jour, and today, of course, we speak of standards.

In regard to accountability measures, standardized exams have been around in the United States since the Industrial Revolution, though the current practice of tying student results to highly punitive measures for schools is most associated with the bipartisan reauthorization of the Elementary and Secondary Education Act (ESEA, also known as No Child Left Behind) in 2001 during the George W. Bush administration. (For a "Brief History of Standardized Testing," see Fletcher, 2009.) "Crisis talk" (Rose, 2009) about the failing state of education has always been with us, too, though it formally moved to the forefront of public consciousness with the 1983 publication of *A Nation at Risk*. This report by the National Commission on Excellence in Education indicted schools for inadequately educating students to the extent that the entire country was falling apart. (See also Berliner & Biddle's 1995 examination of the "manufactured crisis" in American education.)

Broader societal changes have also presented challenges in education. Each era has trumpeted the promise of an educational innovation to transform student learning, be it the slate in the early 1900s, "teaching machines" in the 1960s (Skinner, 1961), the speed-reading machines of the 1970s, or the word processor in the 1980s. The demand to meet the needs of a culturally and linguistically diverse student population has also existed since the first two decades of the twentieth century, when almost nine million immigrants arrived in the United States.

What *is* unprecedented in our current educational era, however, is the simultaneous layering of these challenges and demands. The cultural contexts of learning and teaching have shifted significantly as all of these changes—in standards, punitive accountability measures, rapidly evolving educational tools, and student demographics—are occurring at the same time. Higher academic standards have emerged in national movements such as the Common Core. Punitive measures attached to standardized tests are ever-increasing, most recently linking student performance to teacher "effectiveness" and effectively leading to the abolishment of teacher tenure in many states, including our own, Colorado. Immigration is at a peak in U.S. history: "*More than 7 million people* entered this country in the first five years of the 21st century," and 47 million school-aged children "currently speak a language other than English at home, an increase of 15 million (and up 47%) from 1990" (Rong & Preissle, 2009, emphasis ours). In the meantime, the country as a whole continues to stratify across numerous lines, including race and class (Massey, 2008). Not every development seems insurmountable, however. Excitingly (at least in our view), the digital era has ushered in new tools and participatory social networks that allow both educators and students to collaborate and that support and guide teaching and learning practices publicly and asynchronously (Jenkins et al., 2009). Still, the pressure to "keep up" with these escalating changes is daunting, and thus we collectively wobble.

Admittedly, the notion that a single set of best practices exists to meet this amalgam of challenges is alluring. Yet because the sands beneath teachers' feet are always shifting and because the needs of our students are so idiosyncratic to our individual teaching contexts, the idea seems to us a facile one. In our eyes, these realities make the pose of culturally proactive teaching non-negotiable. Rather than chasing after the holy grail of best practices, then, we believe that a more productive and generative approach to teaching lies in considering the following questions that are intimately tied to this pose:

- How can confronting our own cultural privilege and positionality allow us to better understand the perspectives we carry with us into our classrooms, as well as the voices, questions, and experiences of the students we teach?
- How can we equip our students with critical literacy skills and ourselves with teaching practices necessary for addressing the challenges we've outlined above?
- How can we use these skills and practices to critique and intervene in schools and in a society that is increasingly stratified (Massey, 2008)?

As you will see in the next section, where we describe a recent wobble in our own teaching in relation to these questions, we know from personal experience that there are no definitive answers that will hold for all time. Contexts change, students change, even the questions change, and so must we if we are committed to professional growth. Even though we have been committed to the pose of culturally proactive teaching since we began our careers in high school classrooms, we don't have it all figured out. But because the pose is non-negotiable for us, we continually refer to it as a touchstone for our teaching, and we are always developing strategies that will help us work through wobble toward flow. We offer the following example from our own practice to help you see what an entire P/W/F cycle looks like in relation to the overarching pose of culturally proactive teaching.

WHAT DOES IT LOOK LIKE TO POSE, WOBBLE, FLOW AS A CULTURALLY PROACTIVE TEACHER?: AN EXAMPLE FROM OUR OWN PRACTICE

As educators whose own work is animated by a commitment to this pose, we challenge our preservice teachers to interrogate their positionality and be mindful of how it might shape their teaching practice in the ELA classroom. Though we recognize that each of our students has a distinct identity, our classroom demographics reflect national trends in that the majority of teachers are White, female, and middle-class (Feistritzer, 2011). Yet the students our students will teach are already more racially, culturally, and linguistically diverse than at any other time in our nation's history (Shin & Kominski, 2010; Office of Language, Culture, and Equity, 2011). Herein lies our wobble.

How do we prepare our preservice teachers for this mismatch? How do we address it with the practicing teachers with whom we work? Antero grew up in San Diego and taught at a high school in South Central Los Angeles for 8 years before becoming a professor. As a multiracial, middle-class male, how should he talk about issues of White privilege with the mostly racially homogeneous population of teachers with whom he now works? Cindy is a White, middle-class female who grew up in a small, rural community and taught in large suburban schools in Oklahoma for 11 years. Even though her high school students were more racially diverse than the teachers she works with now, how does she speak with authority about what English language learners need?

These questions moved front and center a couple of years ago when we experienced parallel wobbles in our teaching. On the first day of Antero's Adolescents' Literature course one semester, as he was reviewing the syllabus with students, he explained that they would be examining instances of White privilege that were present in many of the texts he had chosen for the semester. This characteristic is common in the most frequently assigned YA texts and across the industry as a whole (Garcia, 2013). It was at that precise moment that Antero watched the only student of color in the entire class walk out the door. (Later he would learn that she had realized that she sitting in the wrong classroom.) And thus an entire semester of wobble began as Antero stood before the students facilitating an interrogation of White privilege with White students who weren't always aware that they were privileged by virtue of the very fact that they were sitting in a university classroom.

That same semester, Cindy felt that she had been wobbling in a parallel universe in her Teaching Composition class for preservice teachers. Like Antero, she has always foregrounded diversity issues in her teaching. When teaching high school, she had occasionally experienced some pushback from students and their parents whose worldviews were challenged, but she was feeling even more pushback in her university class. While some students were open to interrogating privilege, others felt personally affronted, or sighed, "Here we go again." Still other students expressed exasperation because they saw absolutely no correlation between issues of race and class and the teaching of writing.

Rather than wallow in our respective wobbles, we took some intentional steps to work toward flow. We decided to be more transparent with students about why we were framing our courses with a theoretical focus on issues of privilege and cultural positionality. We also more explicitly linked these concerns to concrete teaching methods so that our students could see how to enact critical pedagogy in their future classrooms. Finally, we implemented several methods to ensure that this approach was threaded throughout the course rather than limited to a handful of class periods. Some of these methods included:

- modeling our own wobble by re-enacting previous discussions we'd had about White privilege and systemic power inequities that get reproduced in schools;
- reading and writing online (in blogs, class forums, on Twitter, etc.) about texts that unapologetically tackle issues of privilege and demonstrate critical pedagogy (e.g., Christensen, 2000, 2009; Delpit, 2006, 2013; Freire & Macedo, 1987; Gartner, 2011; Johnson, 2001);
- interacting online with experienced teachers who constantly inquire into their practice on these issues, including authors of the texts we were reading;
- assigning a service-learning project that required students to develop culturally responsive, digitally robust curriculum focused on the problematic history of our local community related to race relations between Whites and Latinos; and
- sharing our wobble publicly and asking our students to do the same. Cindy documented the entire experience on her personal blog, and for their final as a class, Antero's students created a resource called "Teaching Reading: A Semester of Inquiry" for National Writing Project's Digital Is website (see digitalis.nwp.org/resource/5029).

Meanwhile, the two of us shared our emerging questions with students during class, and also talked, emailed, and texted with one another almost daily about how the classes were shaking out.

These methods bore some resemblance to the culturally proactive methods we had previously used in our high school classrooms, where we:

- asked students to write about their identities and experiences early in the year as a way of building a classroom community that valued diversity;

- deliberately selected texts from a range of authors rather than sticking to the traditional canon with its disproportionate number of White, male, affluent, and heteronormative authors;
- designed assignments and classroom activities to equip students with critical literacy skills they could use to take meaningful social action; and
- widened students' perspectives on social inequities by inviting community members and local experts into the classroom and by using social media to help them connect with others outside of the classroom.

In neither setting, the university nor the high school ELA classroom, has this process been as seamless as it may sound. We still haven't reached satisfactory, once-and-for-all resolutions to our wobbles around culturally proactive teaching, and we undoubtedly never will. Yet we have experienced enough flow moments to deepen our curiosity and commitment. Our questions have gotten smarter, touching off new P/W/F cycles in turn.

We turn to your classroom in the next two sections of the chapter by describing two ways you can enact the pose of culturally proactive teaching: 1) *within* your classroom, by weaving principles of critical pedagogy into your teaching methods, curriculum design, and the learning opportunities you provide for your students; and 2) *beyond* your classroom, by advocating for transformation of inequities present in the education system and even in society at large.

WHAT DOES IT LOOK LIKE TO POSE, WOBBLE, FLOW AS A CULTURALLY PROACTIVE TEACHER *WITHIN* YOUR CLASSROOM?

You assume the pose of culturally proactive teaching when you adopt praxis-oriented imperatives to guide your teaching. Rooted in the foundations of critical pedagogy—as primarily outlined by Paulo Freire (1970)—culturally proactive teaching requires naming, labeling, and *inscribing* the pedagogies you will use to shape your teaching and your students' learning. In this sense, poses are more than nebulous beliefs about the profession that you might state in a teaching philosophy. For example, a statement like *I believe that all students should be treated as individuals*, while admirable, doesn't constitute a culturally proactive pose.

Certainly, poses are often framed by deeply held beliefs like these and should be rooted in sound theory and research, but they are connected more intimately to the daily work of the classroom, and they begin with mindful intent. Just as practitioners of yoga don't just walk into a studio and start "doing yoga" but instead work through a series of named poses that require mindful orientation to the setting at hand, when you adopt poses to ground your practice, you should orient yourself to your classroom context and the needs of the students within it. That is, just as the day-to-day activities of the classroom function as enactments of your intentional poses, the poses you name for yourself should frame day-to-day activities that are consonant with your specific intentions as a teacher.

Using the belief statement mentioned above regarding the value for individual students as an example, you might articulate a more specific culturally proactive pose like *"I will draw on the cultural and linguistic resources my students already possess to support their learning in my classroom."* You could instantiate such a pose by borrowing an assignment from Linda Christensen (2009) that she calls "praise poems"—list poems that call on students to "affirm their right to a place in the world" (p. 28). She describes the assignment in her book *Teaching for Joy and Justice*, which clearly reflects her value for this pose. Although Christensen does not use the term "wobble" in reference to her development of the assignment, it came about due to the disjuncture Christensen often felt between the brilliance and humor she witnessed in her students and the disrespectful and even fearful perceptions that others outside the class held of them, especially the young Black men. She explains that "many people—teachers, parents, reporters, students from other schools—sized up those of us who attended or worked at Jefferson based on stereotyped images and counted us out, usually without ever venturing inside to our classrooms" (pp. 27–28). She developed the "praise poems" assignment as a way of helping her students "talk back" to those with such misconceptions by praising specific aspects of communities to which the students belonged (p. 28).

Christensen explains that she introduces the assignment by reading and discussing with her students a poem called "For My People" by African American poet Margaret Walker (1989). They then emulate Walker's techniques and draft poems celebrating their own communities and countering the misconceptions described above. As students write, Christensen browses around the room and holds mini-conferences with those who need extra support. These teaching methods enact Christensen's pose of drawing on students' cultural and linguistic resources to support their learning by 1) using a poem by an African American woman as a mentor text, 2) helping students identify and celebrate their communities' strengths, and 3) equipping them with language skills and writing processes they can use to express their identities through poetry. Again, though Christensen does not use the language of the P/W/F model, the assignment she developed also addresses the wobble she felt when this pose was directly challenged by others' erroneous misconceptions of her students. Furthermore, it demonstrates the pedagogical moves she made to work toward flow.

As this example shows, some poses emerge from your personal values and the ways you envision your classroom operating. You may also elect to take on poses suggested by other colleagues or published educators, conference speakers, and researchers whose work you admire because doing so pushes your thinking and aligns with your teaching values. We find it helpful to think of these sources not as "experts" (a word that sometimes connotes those with teacher superpowers the rest of us mere mortals will never possess), but as "distant teachers" (John-Steiner, 1997) who hold wisdom you, too, can acquire and act on in your own practice. Feminist and activist educator bell hooks describes Paulo Freire in this similar, touchingly intimate way: "When I discovered the work of the Brazilian thinker Paulo Freire, my first introduction to critical pedagogy, I found a mentor and a guide, someone who understood that learning could be liberatory. With his teachings . . . I began to develop a blueprint for my own pedagogical practice" (1994, p. 6).

Remember that a pose is no less valuable just because you didn't think it up first. In fact, Mikhail Bakhtin (1986) maintains that all our thoughts and words are "filled with *dialogic overtones*. . . . After all, our thought itself—philosophical, scientific, artistic—is born and shaped in the process of interaction and struggle with others' thought" (p. 92). In other words, even the poses we think of as belonging exclusively to us probably carry tinges of others' poses as well. Regardless of whether your poses are original, clearly borrowed, or some amalgam of the two, articulating them is important, because as we pointed out in the previous chapter, poses can function as touchstones to remind yourself of your values, pinpoint what you need to modify or refine, and identify where you need to challenge yourself in order to deepen your practice.

WHAT DOES IT LOOK LIKE TO POSE, WOBBLE, FLOW AS A CULTURALLY PROACTIVE TEACHER *BEYOND* THE CLASSROOM?

As we've described it above, culturally proactive teaching pertains to the everyday transactions that occur between you and your students within your classroom. We argue, however, that it should also extend beyond the confines of your classroom. You become a culturally proactive teacher in this sense when you advocate for educational transformation and when you push back against existing inequitable systems that define teaching and learning in narrow ways. Admittedly this is a tall order, especially when you feel like you're operating in continual survival mode, as new teachers often do. We thus want to emphasize that many small moves—like sharing articles with colleagues, commenting on education blogs, participating in Twitter chats about educational issues, joining organizations like the National Council of Teachers of English, and participating in local workshops—can help you enact your agency and make an impact on the profession even at early stages in your career.

Many teachers we know, new and experienced alike, feel as if they are in constant danger of "being posed" in today's educational climate, much like the dolls or action figures you probably played with as a child; that is, their agency as teachers is challenged on a regular basis. Some are pressured to teach to the test by following a one-size-fits-all curriculum. Some have little if any say in the texts they teach. The list goes on. Regardless of where we teach or how long we've been teaching, all of us operate within systems larger and longer-standing than ourselves. It's easy to feel powerless when the systems in which we teach make demands on us and our students that may not coincide with our views on teaching and learning. While it's sometimes possible to work within the constraints of your department or school, local systems like these are inevitably nested within larger systems that can seem impossible to negotiate, much less to critique, restructure, or downright oppose. When you feel as if you are being posed, and you can be sure that at some point you will, what should you do? How do you keep teaching in ways that don't compromise your principles?

The first step in working through this wobble is acknowledging that you *always* teach on contested ground because schooling is such a complex enterprise with so many stakeholders involved; nevertheless, you want to advocate for more powerful and humane approaches to teaching and learning. To be clear, we are not suggesting that you blatantly disregard federal mandates or the rules and expectations of your school and district. After all, you have to keep your job or you won't have an impact on students at all. We still believe, however, that teachers aren't Barbie dolls or action figures (action heroes, maybe).

Staunch proponents of practitioner research, Marilyn Cochran-Smith and Susan Lytle, maintain that teachers can act as "deliberative intellectuals who constantly theorize practice as part of practice itself" (2009, p. 2), but a far too common characterization of teachers these days is that they are deprofessionalized "technicians" (Giroux, 2012), who must be "trained" to implement scripted, all-purpose curriculum written by supposed experts outside of the classroom primarily for the purpose of achieving high scores on standardized tests. As we mentioned previously, the No Child Left Behind Act (NCLB) in 2001 furthered an era of accountability under the guise of educational improvement. Unfortunately, accountability measures have been punitively enforced when test scores aren't within required ranges. These misguided efforts have narrowed opportunities for student learning and have resulted in almost constant teacher evaluation and the tying of job security to student test scores (Brick, 2012; Meier, 2003; Ravitch, 2010).

Given these circumstances, you may be thinking that posing proactively is easier said than done. As an early career teacher, how can you possibly be expected to take on or take down today's overly regulated system? The answer is that you as one individual most likely won't be able to do so. In his 2014 address at the National Council of Teachers of English conference, outgoing President Ernest Morrell noted that the complicated part about engaging in advocacy is "having the courage to do it. You can't do it alone." Yet he urged the audience to remember that we as English teachers are uniquely qualified for advocacy because we are readers, writers, and communicators by trade. By joining with others who share a culturally pro-active pose on teaching, our impact can be substantial in moving education forward.

In fact, advocacy is a core value of professional organizations like the National Council of Teachers of English (NCTE) and the National Writing Project (NWP). Both have state and local affiliates, so if you haven't done so already, you should get connected right away. In addition to providing first-rate resources for English teachers through conferences and publica-tions, NCTE offers opportunities for collective advocacy, including updates on current issues and policies related to literacy instruction and student learning; anti-censorship efforts; the creation of resolutions and position statements teachers can use to inform public policy; and annual visits to Washington, DC, where teachers voice their concerns to legislators. The National Writing Project, the longest-standing professional network de-voted to the improvement of writing in schools, likewise states on their website (www.nwp.org) that "collectively, teacher-leaders are our greatest resource for educational reform." Since its founding in 1974, NWP's advo-cacy efforts have been guided by the principle that "access to high-quality educational experiences is a basic right of all learners and a cornerstone of equity." Since the very start of our respective careers, we've been active in both organizations. Both have supported our development as teacher advo-cates and have given us the courage Ernest Morrell describes. We recognize that we are part of a collective movement determined to lead the profession forward in ways that will ultimately create a more just and peaceful world.

Again, we intentionally characterize this forward action as *proactive* rather than embedded in the notion of "educational reform." We believe there's a place for the latter term, but we sometimes find it problematic. Even the structure of the word—"re-form"—suggests revising an already es-tablished system by building on what has come before. To be sure, pushing back against chafing professional constraints and having a historical context for present work can also shape an alternative vision for the future. In fact, we ourselves have been committed to educational reform efforts throughout our careers.

But we are adamant in our view that educational *transformation* is possible and necessary if we are to meet the unprecedented challenges and opportunities of the fast-paced 21st century that we described earlier in this chapter. Furthermore, as we explain in more detail in Chapter 3 on civic lit-eracy, we see potential for the work we do in school (which is the one social mechanism all of us share in common as citizens) to disrupt the inequities caused by the continual stratification of our country as a whole (Briggs, 2005; Massey, 2008; Orfield, 2002). These realities call for new visions and radical change, rather than re-forming an established system that is rapidly becoming archaic.

Some teachers worry that advocacy practices like these have no place in the classroom or in their careers. We often hear our students saying things like, "I don't feel comfortable bringing my political agenda into the classroom," or "My job is to teach English, not to involve students in cultural critique," or "It's way too risky to disrupt the status quo. What if I lose my job?" But there's no such thing as an apolitical position in teaching. Choosing not to disrupt the status quo is itself a political choice. In fact, we see it as a capitulation. In this heavily mandated era when it seems that being posed is the only option, adopting a culturally proactive pose in your teaching is not only a subversive act (Postman & Weingartner, 1971), but a moral imperative. Yes, educational transformation is a gargantuan task, but making even small moves makes a difference. Yes, you will wobble, but you don't have to go it alone. By bolstering yourself with the support of research and larger professional networks, and by banding together with other forward-thinking colleagues, you can work your way toward collective moments of flow. In so doing, you claim agency to transform education and challenge inequitable educational and social structures that would limit your students' access to meaningful learning and richer lives.

CONCLUSION

Bob Fecho points out that any time teachers aspire toward growth, "the idea is not to achieve perfection, but to *incline toward perfection*" (2011, p. 103; emphasis ours). This is especially true for the pose of culturally proactive teaching. Rather than see it as a state of being you will eventually achieve, recognize that it is a process of becoming. It will require you to engage in continual P/W/F cycles, lest you fall into a business-as-usual mode in your teaching or into the trap of talking the talk of culturally proactive teaching without walking the walk. As Van Lier (2004) cautions, "Critical language education should be neither proselytizing nor indoctrinating, because then it basically ceases to be critical, it just becomes dogma, and dogma controls thought and action, and that is not being critical" (p. 189). It may also be helpful to consider this tenet of yoga, which is equally applicable to teaching:

> Yoga is a journey and a process; it is not a destination or a competition. There is no goal to achieve besides being completely present with where you are in your practice. Accept your body's limitations and honor what it can and can't do, but don't let that be an excuse to minimize what you can achieve (Burgin, 2012, Ch. 7, para. 1).

In the remainder of this book we explore five other poses that we believe contribute to a culturally proactive approach to teaching. As you read, we encourage you to apply these poses to your own practice, take up the Pose, Wobble, Flow model, and challenge yourself to follow Fecho's advice and "incline toward perfection."

PROVOCATIONS

1. In his book *Shut Up and Listen: Teaching Writing That Counts in Urban Schools*, educator Christopher Knaus deliberately identifies his cultural positionality as a White, middle-class male and describes how it shapes his practice. In doing so, he notes, "To not spend my life challenging the racism our schools promotes [sic] is to accept White privilege and the racial order that silences the world around me. This is not the world I want to live in" (2011, p. 44). Considering this claim, does your practice reflect the world you want to live in? If not, what are you willing to do about it?

2. The unspoken effects of privilege and oppression in schools and society pervade the lived identities of our students. Given this, what perspectives on the world does your teaching enable? What does it normalize? What does it disrupt?

3. In her essay "White Privilege: Unpacking the Invisible Knapsack," Peggy McIntosh makes a list of the daily privileges she carries in her cultural knapsack (or backpack) as a White, middle-class woman. Some of these items include being able to buy Band-Aids that match the color of her skin, routinely seeing people of her race featured in television and other media, and never being asked to represent her entire racial group. If you were to make a list of what you carry in your cultural backpack, what items would you include? What about your students' backpacks? How do these items reflect or deflect the privilege you do or do not experience on a daily basis?

4. Looking at your answers to the question above, how will you acknowledge, problematize, and address your privilege within the classroom? In what ways can you make these practices clear to your own students?

5. While these questions have primarily teased out your own positionality, how can you best learn about and engage the cultural identities of your students? What questions will you ask? What nonverbal cues within your classroom will signal to your students that you are creating a culturally proactive environment for them?

CONNECTIONS

Explore the following resources for further insight into culturally proactive teaching:

McIntosh, Peggy. (2005). *White Privilege: Unpacking the Invisible Knapsack.*

> This seminal text on contemporary White privilege is primarily an accessible list of forms of privilege that often go unacknowledged. This is a useful text for reflecting on your own privileges and the ways these do or do not get reinforced within your classroom.

Johnson, Allan. (2001). *Privilege, Power, and Difference.*

> This oft-used text in teacher education programs clearly identifies strategies that those with privilege can use to shape more democratic, diverse classroom spaces. In particular, we often have students fill out their own "Diversity Wheel" found in the book as an instructive exercise to take inventory of their positionality.

Christensen, Linda. *Reading, Writing, and Rising Up* (2000) and *Teaching for Joy and Justice* (2009).

> These books offer clear teaching strategies and classroom examples of ELA instruction that is culturally proactive.

CHAPTER 2

Hacking the English Language Arts
What It Means to Be a Vulnerable Learner

The term "hacking" has a checkered past and has commonly been associated with criminal activity (i.e., hacking into a computer with malicious intent). Yet on his educational blog, budtheteacher.com, Bud Hunt contends that hacking should be an "essential [lens] for any learner's toolbag, be that learner a student in a classroom, or one who frames the learning of others." He points out that "[learning] happens when we hack things . . . because we must understand what our situation is, and how we can fiddle with it, in order to improve it" (2012).

We agree. Thinking of yourself as a hacker—of traditional notions of teaching and learning, of curriculum, and of educational systems at large—can help you claim and retain a sense of agency that may feel all too elusive during your first few years of teaching. This pose can keep you from seeing yourself and your students as no more than cogs in a system beyond your control. It reminds you of your capacity to survey the system you and your students are inhabiting and then, in Bud's words, figure how to "fiddle with it, in order to improve it."

The pose of Teacher as Hacker is a logical extension of the overarching pose of culturally proactive teaching that has been central to our and many other educators' attempts to "fiddle with" the educational system. As William Ayers and Ryan Alexander-Tanner (2010) visually depict in *To Teach: The Journey, in Comics*, this traditional system has typically positioned the teacher as "master and commander of the ship, poised with complete confidence, in charge and in control" of fearful, compliant students (p. 2). In *Pedagogy of the Oppressed*, however, Freire (1970) describes a different vision:

> To be a good liberating educator, you need above all to have faith in human beings. You need to love. You must be convinced that the fundamental effort of education is to help with the liberation of people, never their domestication. You must be convinced that when people reflect on their domination they begin a first step in changing their relationship to the world. (p. 62)

Freire's words, first published in Portuguese in 1968, are at least as relevant today as they were when he shared them with literacy educators in the 1960s. Freire proposed an alternative model for schooling apart from the traditional banking model wherein teachers deposit knowledge that students must passively consume, then withdraw and return to the teacher upon demand. Rather, in Freire's model of *praxis* (i.e., critical reflection that leads to transformative action), teachers and students pose problems relevant to their experiences and jointly construct knowledge in their pursuit of answers. As Shor explains it, "Knowing, to Freire, means being an active subject who questions and transforms. To learn is to recreate the way we see ourselves, our education, and our society" (1993, p. 25).

The pose of Teacher as Hacker is situated in this dialogic model. By hacking the traditional banking approach to education, teachers disrupt the commonplace view that they are *the* sole experts in the classroom. Admittedly, stepping off this imaginary pedestal as a teacher can be a frightening prospect; there's comfort in feeling as if you can call the shots in the classroom because you are the one in charge. We maintain, however, that this confidence is imaginary and limiting for both us and our students. By taking on the pose of Teacher as Hacker, you can be a powerful model for your students that learning involves vulnerability, uncertainty, and change.

TEACHER AS HACKER: CREATE AND SUSTAIN A DIALOGIC CURRICULUM THAT MEETS STUDENTS' LEARNING NEEDS BY:

➤ cultivating a classroom environment that enables vulnerable learning;

➤ emphasizing a production-oriented view of learning that positions students as "makers"; and

➤ critically reading one's teaching context and pushing back against systemic constraints that might limit students' learning.

VULNERABLE LEARNING, VULNERABLE TEACHING

In an interview Cindy conducted with former high school English teacher Danielle Filipiak, Danielle describes one of the key aspects of the Teacher as Hacker pose: *vulnerable learning*, which we define as an inquiry-driven process that engages both intellect and emotion, resulting in impact on the learner and her or his world. While it's easy to imagine how this process is worthwhile for students, Danielle points out that vulnerable learning is equally important for teachers:

> I think that for me to show students that I'm a person who has questions that I don't have answers to yet, it kind of lets students know that collectively, we have the potential to ask and then go about answering together questions that matter to us, and kind of sharing in that tension that exists in that space that stands between how you wish things would be and how they are.

Some of the most profound learning experiences Cindy has had to this day occurred in her middle school science class, where her teacher, Mr. Hougardy, modeled precisely the kind of vulnerable learning Danielle describes and fostered it in his students as well. Looking back, Cindy recognizes that he was a teacher-hacker extraordinaire due to the classroom environment he established and the teaching methods he employed within it. In the conservative rural community where Cindy grew up, Mr. Hougardy was always in trouble, partly because his eccentricities spilled over into his teaching, but mostly because he didn't shy away from controversy and insisted that his students question everything about how the world worked and why. As Cindy and her classmates left his classroom each day, he reminded them to look up at the one-word poster above his door. It read "THINK," and so they did.

Cindy and her peers found Mr. Hougardy's class to be a vibrant academic mecca—one of the few spaces in the school where questions were taken seriously, and it was okay to ask them (even though he rarely answered them outright, much to their irritation). In fact, Mr. Hougardy was a question machine. Although he wasn't an English teacher, he left a vivid and lasting impression on Cindy because he hacked to pieces just about every assumption and practice related to traditional approaches to teaching and learning. Rather than professing what he or a textbook writer considered the essential body of scientific facts every middle schooler should memorize and recite, he guided, supported, and facilitated their budding attempts at scientific *inquiry*.

On a regular basis, Cindy and her classmates witnessed Mr. Hougardy voicing genuine questions he couldn't definitively answer at that point in time. He posed, he wobbled, he flowed, and the expectation and invitation of his teaching was that students do the same. In doing so, he disrupted the notion that the teacher is *the* expert in the room, but established that anyone, students included, could become more expert by exercising the iterative processes that scientists use to make sense of the world: inquiring, observing, reading relevant texts, writing to understand, collecting and analyzing data, acting on their newfound knowledge, then inquiring once again. They learned about water quality by studying the aquatic life present in Mason jars of pond water they scooped from the nearest farm. For her science fair project, Cindy examined lichen growth on trees in wooded areas to determine the effects of emissions from the local power plant. Because Mr. Hougardy himself was a vulnerable learner, he made his classroom a place where vulnerable learning could occur.

His approach to teaching and learning cultivated an environment where students could develop the following key dispositions enacted by vulnerable learners who, with the support of teachers, peers, and knowledgeable others:

- know how to engage, co-construct, and pursue questions of consequence that are illuminated by course content and that matter within and beyond their local context;

- use literacy skills and strategies tools in the service of inquiry by consulting, collecting, interpreting, composing, and sharing texts that support and demonstrate their learning;
- are personally invested and collaboratively inclined because they value the perspectives and expertise of others for sharpening their thinking;
- are unwilling to play it safe. Relentlessly curious and open to change, they are compelled to experiment, risk failure, and persist through difficulty to deepen their understanding; and
- take action armed with the knowledge they have constructed. They examine, critique, and push back against systemic constraints that inhibit a more habitable, just, and peaceful world.

We suspect that because the intellectual dimension of these behaviors is apparent, you are likely to see them as right up the teacher's alley. At the same time, you may be wondering why we have chosen to refer to learning as a "vulnerable" experience, rather than using more common terms like "authentic" or "lifelong." By doing so, we mean to convey that learning refers to more than intellectual growth. Rather, because learning entails wobbling, emotions are also at play. H. G. Wells is credited with saying, "You have learned something. That always feels at first as if you had lost something." And indeed, learning does involve a kind of loss in learners' transitions from questioning what they think they know, to a state of "not-knowing" (Barthelme, 1997), to the alteration of previously existing views.

Barthelme views "not-knowing" as an essential part of creativity: "The not-knowing is crucial to art, is what permits art to be made. Without the scanning process engendered by not-knowing, without the possibility of having the mind move in unanticipated directions, there would be no invention" (p. 12). Although he refers to artistic production here, we believe Barthelme's idea of "not-knowing" also applies to the vulnerability inherent in constructing knowledge and demonstrating one's learning. He insists that "[p]roblems are a comfort" (p. 14) because solving them results in richly significant products. "Problems in part define the kind of work the writer [and we would add, *teacher*] chooses to do"; thus they "are not to be avoided but embraced" (p. 18).

Teachers who foster vulnerable learning create classrooms where "not-knowing" (Barthelme, 1997) is the norm; thus it isn't entirely accurate to say that they "empower" their students. Rather, just as Cindy's middle school science teacher did, they create conditions in which students can claim and exercise their own power as learners, primarily because these teachers are vulnerable learners themselves. In a classroom full of 12-year-olds, this is no minor feat, but because these teachers understand firsthand the process of posing and pursuing meaningful questions that address shared concerns, they hold confidence that their students can do the same. They communicate this confidence by concocting a strange and marvelous brew that blends student questions, required course content, and local concerns, often with global impact.

Their classrooms are safe places, but not because they are absent of conflict and controversy. Instead, teachers who foster an environment conducive to vulnerable learning recognize that such energy-laden moments often indicate that students are wobbling toward what Lee Anne Bell (2010) calls the "learning edge":

> The concepts of *comfort zone* and *learning edge* [are] tools for tuning in to one's own feelings and reactions as well as for paying attention to others in the room. *Comfort zone* refers to playing it safe and holding on to what is comfortable and therefore not challenging. *Learning edge* refers to taking risks to consider new perspectives and ideas. [Use] these concepts to push [your] learning edge and consciously take risks to learn something new. (p. 96).

In taking students to the learning edge, teachers who value vulnerable learning intentionally combine structures—physical and interactional—and equip students with literacy routines that result in "safe-to" environments where learners take risks together, rather than "safe-from" environments intended to suppress potential discomfort caused by the shifts that vulnerable learning requires (Fecho, Collier, Friese, & Wilson, 2010). In an interview Cindy conducted with former high school English teacher Nicole Mirra, Nicole points out that although vulnerable learning can be "a scary process, . . . it can also be really transformative and powerful and amazing." She emphasizes that relationship-building, modeling, and patience were key methods she drew upon to hack traditional "test-based, accountability forms of learning" that require nothing more than "regurgitating information on a test and then forgetting about it." She explains:

> I feel like I always had to start with relationships and trust-building and allowing myself to be vulnerable and try to change students' ideas that they sometimes came into class with from previous teachers—that the teacher is the holder of all authority and all knowledge and all perfection, and show that I fail and that my ideas change when I learn from them—or when I hear something that I didn't think of before, that I can make mistakes. So it takes a while. It definitely takes a few months into the school year before I think they're really with me on that because I think you're breaking out of a pretty traditional and powerful way of teaching that a lot of people use.

This kind of teaching requires extensive modeling, norming (and re-norming) with students, and "perpetual scaffolding" (O'Donnell-Allen, 2011). To clarify the last term, though scaffolding is often seen as a front-loading process, merely prepping students for vulnerable learning experiences, while important, just isn't enough. To increase the likelihood that they will transfer their knowledge and skills to future contexts, students need ongoing support from teachers and peers, combined with opportunities for reflection throughout the learning process. For example, in instances when Nicole's students resisted vulnerable learning, she often asked them to pause and reflect on the source of their discomfort:

> I try to talk to students when they're in that moment, maybe getting them to think . . . , "Do you really like it when teachers tell you what to do all the time?" Just kind of interrogating that, but not in a like disciplining way, but like a genuine curiosity of, "Why is it so much easier when we're told what to do?" Because you don't have to use all of your brain or all the parts of your heart to actually get invested in this. You kind of do a mechanistic kind of routine. I think I can get deeper into those conversations with students when I get to know them and they get to know me and that I'm not trying to frustrate them or give them a task that is impossible to complete.

We've also found that high school students aren't the only ones who wobble when their teachers hack traditional approaches to learning. In fact, some of our preservice teachers also view the idea that teachers should be vulnerable learners to be unsettling. They know what roles teachers and students should occupy, they know to "do school," and this isn't it. In one ELA methods course Cindy was teaching, the class was divided over whether or not classrooms should be sites for vulnerable learning. This disagreement made itself abundantly clear in the wobbling Cindy and her students experienced throughout the semester to establish a viable classroom community.

At the beginning of the course, Cindy used the same method that she has always used throughout her high school and university teaching, asking students to devise classroom norms to guide their daily interactions and help form a supportive learning community. To do so, she facilitated a whole-class discussion around the following questions, which ask students not only to develop broad norms, but also to imagine what these will look like in actual practice:

- What norms should govern our classroom community and our whole-class interactions with one another? What will it look like/feel like/sound like when things are going well?
- What (additional) guidelines should govern our small-group discussions and collaborative work in general? What will it look like/feel like/sound like when things are going well?
- How will we hold each other accountable if the above norms start breaking down?

During the semester at hand, the norms the class created—which included everything from turn-taking in class discussion, to holding one another accountable for work on collaborative projects—reflected a (presumably) shared commitment to sustaining a classroom atmosphere that supported vulnerable learning. Despite these laudable norms, however, several incidents of disrespect occurred, including one that bordered on bullying. Even after a formal class meeting of the kind Cindy used to have with her high school students to revisit norms and reiterate her zero-tolerance policy for such behavior, the nagging dynamics remained to the end of the semester.

In a final attempt to intervene, Cindy asked students to engage in a silent discussion about vulnerable learning related to the book they were reading at the time, Meenoo Rami's *Thrive* (2014). She pasted quotations she had selected from the assigned reading onto sheets of butcher paper and set them on tables around the room. The class then browsed the quotes, responding anonymously to the quotations and to one another's comments on sticky notes before having a verbal discussion to debrief their ideas. Although Rami doesn't use the term "vulnerable learning," the quotations Cindy selected from *Thrive* describe the importance of creating joyful classrooms where students demonstrate personal investment in their learning. Rami also emphasizes that in order to thrive professionally, teachers, especially new teachers, must recognize that learning is a nonstop process that benefits from support by colleagues, mentors, and professional networks.

In the prompts Cindy wrote for the silent discussion, she asked students to consider whether or not their current classroom felt like a joyful place to learn and to think about how they would make their future classrooms joyful places to learn. One student circled the word "vulnerable" and commented, "Seems to be the heart of the debate." Comments from other students revealed that this was indeed the case:

- "Why *vulnerable*? It has a negative connotation. Learning should be enjoyable, not risky."
- "Why should we be vulnerable in a college classroom? Completely different scenarios than secondary classrooms." (A nearby sticky note in response to this comment read, "AGREE!!")
- "Vulnerable learning means making mistakes that create learning experiences. How do we become okay with mistakes? Failure?"
- "Rami also says that to have vulnerable learning, you also need to show bits and pieces of your own vulnerable learning. I think our class has done a good job of this for the most part. It has been stressful at times but it's school, so that's expected."

As these examples show, the preservice teachers in Cindy's course expressed strong opinions, questions, and doubts about the viability of vulnerable learning in the present methods class and in their future classrooms. The final comment above is especially telling. For us, this comment suggests that stress is an expected byproduct of attempting to be a vulnerable learner in school because doing so bucks the norm. In traditional educational models, "not-knowing" (Barthelme, 1997) is often seen as a sign of intellectual weakness or even unwillingness to accept received knowledge from textbooks and lecturing teachers (Ayers & Alexander-Tanner, 2010). If this is the case, then teaching in ways that enable vulnerable learning requires considerable hacking of:

1. traditional models of teaching and learning that historically privilege teacher authority over student agency;
2. notions that knowledge is fixed and thus learning is recitative, as reflected in scripted curriculum and traditional teaching methods that require rote demonstrations of learning;
3. misguided assumptions, as embedded in educational policy related to student achievement (e.g., NCLB legislation), that literacy consists of a set of easily measurable skills rather than a collection of inquiry-oriented tools that enable meaningful action; and
4. facile views that classrooms should be "safe spaces" that avoid conflict and controversy in favor of minimizing the discomfort students are likely to feel when their thinking is challenged (see Fecho, Collier, Friese, & Wilson, 2010).

As Nicole Mirra pointed out earlier, these ideas are so embedded in the educational system that students are likely to resist your efforts to hack them. Although their reactions will almost certainly cause you to wobble as a result, you can learn from the examples of other experienced teachers who have experienced flow in their attempts to support vulnerable learning. In Cindy's account of her middle school experiences in Mr. Hougardy's science class, you saw the lasting impact caused by a teacher who unabashedly modeled vulnerable learning and established conditions that allowed his students to experience it as well. Likewise, Nicole pointed out the importance of modeling, building relationships with students over time, and pausing in moments of resistance to help them reflect on their thinking in order to recognize the transformative potential of vulnerable learning. Finally, in the example of Cindy's university classroom, you saw a method of helping students establish classroom norms that she has generally found to be successful in fostering a class culture where vulnerable learning can take place, albeit not in the particular instance described above. Even in that difficult class, however, Cindy found that the silent discussion method she used allowed more reticent students to share views and questions that may have been more difficult to voice in a verbal class discussion.

In addition to these methods, perhaps the most important thing to remember as you work toward flow is that creating this kind of environment is essential for helping students thrive not just in your classroom, but also in their lives. As Danielle Filipiak so aptly pointed out in our interview with her on vulnerable learning:

Everybody needs a place to be able to struggle as a person, to struggle through who they are, especially when you're an adolescent. . . . [Students] can learn anything you want from the Internet, so why go to school? You're also going to school to learn how to be a better human being, so if the adults around you do not permit you to do that, then that's a problem, right? Because then you're coming out of this experience that you've had for the first 13 years of your life not practicing being a better human being. And people say that's left up to home, but I disagree. It's up to all of us. And so if that's going to be an endeavor we take on, then vulnerability is a necessary part because you can't fail otherwise.

VIEWING STUDENTS AS MAKERS
BY HARNESSING THE POWER OF
CONNECTED LEARNING

Our discussion of vulnerable learning thus far has focused primarily on hacking the traditional banking model of education that positions students as passive *recipients* of information dispensed by the teacher as all-knowing expert (Freire, 1970). In this section, we shift our focus to the second aspect of the Teacher as Hacker pose, which emphasizes a production-centered view of learning that repositions students as *makers* of artifacts they value while at the same time developing their literacy practices.

This idea takes its cue from the burgeoning, grassroots, worldwide Maker Movement, which is rooted in the assumption that humans have an inherent need to create meaningful material objects. Local iterations of the Maker Movement can be seen in community "makerspaces," informal, physical workspaces where makers come together, united by a spirit of creative play, to create things and share materials and equipment like 3D printers and power saws. Collaboration is a key aspect of makerspaces, as makers informally seek out and share one another's expertise, solve design problems together, and sometimes work on joint projects. On a broader scale, the movement's popularity is evident at Makerfaires, festivals in large cities where do-it-yourselfers can learn new skills and share the things they've made.

The founder of Makerfaires, Dale Dougherty, is often credited with conceptualizing the movement in the United States. He describes the "maker mindset" as follows:

Makers have a sense of what they can do and what they can learn to do. Like artists, they are motivated by internal goals, not extrinsic rewards. They are inspired by the work of others. Most importantly, they do not wait until the future to create and make. They feel an urgency to do something now—or lose the opportunity to do it at all. (n.d., p. 1)

In linking the ethos of the maker mindset to teaching, we ask you to consider what happens when you replace the word "maker" in the last quotation with "student." What shifts would be necessary in a traditional classroom if students were to approach learning in these ways? How would the power dynamics shift? How would the relationships change between you and your students? Between them and their peers? What are the implications for your instructional design? Your answers to these questions should make it clear that cultivating a maker mindset in your students requires you to take a production-oriented approach to learning.

We and many other educators have found an approach to education called "connected learning" to be a powerful tool for reconceptualizing the classroom in these ways. As researcher Mimi Ito and her colleagues (2013) define it,

> Connected learning is realized when a young person is able to pursue a personal interest or passion with the support of friends and caring adults, and is in turn able to link this learning and interest to academic achievement, career success or civic engagement. This model is based on evidence that the most resilient, adaptive, and effective learning involves individual interest as well as social support to overcome adversity and provide recognition. (p. 4)

Connected learning shares many of the features of making described above in that it is focused on production and actively driven by learners' interests. Connected learners collaborate and share resources with peers and others and often use digital tools to leverage their learning. Beyond these similarities with making, however, connected learning is undergirded by a focus on equity and access, especially for nondominant youth. By drawing on and expanding youth knowledge and expertise, it intentionally incorporates academic learning and civic engagement. In sum, connected learning occurs in the sweet spot where youth interests, peer culture, and academic needs intersect. The connected learning model was originally developed in informal education contexts located primarily outside of the school day, like libraries, community centers, after-school programs, and nonprofit organizations. Yet we also have seen compelling evidence (including in our own classrooms) that connected learning isn't limited to out-of-school contexts.

To draw attention to what connected learning looks like in school, Antero spearheaded an ebook called *Teaching in the Connected Learning Classroom* (2014) and co-curated it with Cindy, Danielle Filipiak, Nicole Mirra, Bud Hunt, and our colleague Cliff Lee, a teacher educator in California. All of us are former high school English teachers and Connected Learning Ambassadors for the National Writing Project (NWP). Together we curated a set of classroom examples of connected learning from an

NWP website called Digital Is that explores and exemplifies "what it means to learn and teach writing in our increasingly digital and interconnected world" (digitalis.nwp.org). Each chapter of the book features vignettes, written mostly by classroom teachers, that flesh out one of six key elements of connected learning. Table 2.1 describes each element and provides a brief classroom example of connected learning from the book, as well as links to related resources on Digital Is.

In these and the many other vignettes featured in *Teaching in the Connected Learning Classroom* (Garcia, 2014b), educators across grade levels and diverse contexts demonstrate how the principles of connected learning can be harnessed to support students in the process of making artifacts they care about. Doing so calls on students to engage a range of literacy skills for the purpose of critiquing and redressing inequities in their local contexts and, in many cases, the world at large. To get a closer look at how this looks in the classroom, let's zoom in on one of the thumbnails from Table 2.1.

Texas teacher Jennifer Woollven embarked on a project with her high school students to examine media coverage of their "typical, struggling urban school" as she describes it in her Digital Is resource. Using the *shared purpose* principle of connected learning, they united around the common cause of improving their school's reputation, which was often demeaned in scathing editorials published by the local newspaper. To challenge these negative views, students gathered examples of the positive opportunities and accomplishments at their school, shared the resource with local media outlets, and made a formal request for more positive coverage (which they indeed got when one of the harshest columnists transformed into an advocate). When their school faced the danger of being turned into a charter, students wrote letters, staged protests, spoke at school board meetings, and ultimately were instrumental in getting the decision reversed. In Woollven's words, "[they] had a shared purpose, they had encouraging teachers and mentors, but most importantly, they discovered the power of using their voices to tell their story and ultimately to impact the story of their community." In short, they made an assemblage of literacy artifacts in order to make a difference.

Jennifer and the other teachers featured in these examples, like teachers everywhere, are required to meet standards, administer state tests, and meet other mandates that don't always honor their students as learners. Some of them teach in schools on academic watch and are expected to work within a narrow, prescribed curriculum. Yet they have succeeded in implementing curricular elements that embody the philosophy of making and enable their students to really direct their own learning. Drawing on the principles of connected learning has helped them maintain an unstinting view of their students as makers, and even though they might not use this exact term, we daresay they see themselves as makers as well.

Table 2.1. Classroom Examples of the Six Elements of Connected Learning

Connected Learning Element	Description	Classroom Example and Link to the Digital Is Resource
Interest-driven learning	"A concept based in the seemingly common-sense notion that students will gain more knowledge and skills at higher levels of intellectual rigor when their learning originates from issues or activities that innately captivate them" (Mirra, 2014, p. 10)	Meenoo Rami's high school students work in teams to produce and publish an online zine on self-selected topics relevant to local teens in Philadelphia. **Link:** digitalis.nwp.org/resource/3616
Peer-supported learning	Foregrounds youth voice and occurs when "young people fluidly contribute, share, and give feedback in inclusive social experiences" (O'Donnell-Allen, 2014, p. 25)	For a multiliteracies project in a course on teaching reading, Antero Garcia's preservice English teachers collaborate to create a Digital Is resource that expands narrow definitions of literacy, problematizes inequitable power structures in schooling, and provides resources for teaching reading to adolescents. **Link:** digitalis.nwp.org/resource/5029
Academically oriented learning	Emphasizes the connections between academic study and "civic and work-based life-learning that . . . [allows] students to be able to thrive and shape society in the future" (Garcia, 2014a, p. 53)	Working in a 1:1 laptop school, Larissa Pahomov's high school students write and receive feedback on biweekly essays that address the question "Why is the world the way that it is?" Housed on Google Docs, the assignment template provides space for rough and final drafts, peer editing, a rubric, teacher comments, and student reflection. **Link:** digitalis.nwp.org/resource/2738

Connected Learning Element	Description	Classroom Example and Link to the Digital Is Resource
Production-centered classrooms	Contexts for learning that "support and encourage creating, remixing, sharing, and curating of personally meaningful work" (Lee, 2014, p. 57) through "production of [artifacts] with a clear purpose and with an authentic audience in mind" (p. 69)	Danielle Filipiak's students in an urban Title I high school produce a range of media artifacts, including digital self-portraits and photojournalism projects on community issues, that address "powerful essential questions whose answers had a direct impact on the trajectory of their lives" (p. 65). **Link:** digitalis.nwp.org/resource/3400
Openly networked learning experiences	Employ tools (often but not always digital) that connect students' "interests and passions . . . across contexts, locations, and institutions" and allow them to "[share] their learning in ways that [make] it accessible to others" (Hunt, 2014, p. 72)	Gail Desler, a district technology coordinator for a low-income suburban district, connects elementary and middle school students using tools like blogs, VoiceThread, online discussions, and videoconferencing to build a community of "change writers" exploring topics like tolerance, bullying, and genocide. The online community has grown into a network that includes teachers, K-12 students, and community activists across California. **Link:** digitalis.nwp.org/resource/272
Learning around a shared purpose	Focuses on "the purposes and interests that matter most to students, . . . [equips] youth to be more critical, confident, and resourceful human beings in the present" (p. 87), and results in "[o]utcomes like resistance, resilience, and interconnected relationships" (Filipiak, 2014, p. 89)	Jennifer Woollven's urban high students employ a range of traditional literacy practices and digital tools as they unite around a common purpose—improving the reputation of their struggling high school in the eyes of the community and ultimately preventing the closure of their school. **Link:** digitalis.nwp.org/resource/5426

TEACHING WITH A MAKER MINDSET: DESIGNING
INNOVATIVE CURRICULUM TO HACK LIMITING CONSTRAINTS

In the slam poem "What Teachers Make" (2006), teacher Taylor Mali is at a dinner party when a condescending guest suggests that teachers' subpar salaries reflect a reality that "those who can't do, teach." The remainder of the poem functions as Mali's rebuttal of this misguided assumption. Rather than revealing his salary figure, Mali lists the actions he consistently takes as a teacher: calling parents, teaching students to work hard, to read, write, and critically question. Together, these actions allow him to achieve his most important goal: making a difference.

This is a familiar goal to most teachers. In fact, we don't know a single teacher who chose the profession with the guiding purpose of helping students bubble in the correct answers on standardized tests. Rather, like Taylor Mali, they take the long view that "schooling should be a humanizing process" (Filipiak, 2014, p. 87). Although policymakers give lip service to this goal, in reality, it often recedes into the background because it isn't a "measurable" outcome. We concur with Mali, however, that every action teachers take on a daily basis—building positive relationships with students, holding high expectations for them, and providing meaningful learning opportunities—hinges on a desire to make a difference. This is why teachers must act courageously to hack existing, reductive systems that might stunt students' learning. This is why we must see ourselves as makers, too. In addition to enacting the important relational aspects of teaching, seeing yourself as a maker also pertains to the nuts and bolts of your practice. Remember how in a previous section we asked you to apply Dougherty's description of the "maker mindset" to students? Taking on a maker mindset yourself transforms routine responsibilities like writing lesson plans into opportunities for play and creativity, or rather, as we like to think about it, for "uncreative teaching."

We refer to "uncreative teaching" as the process of constructing, making, repurposing, and tinkering with instructional materials, often with the collaborative support of colleagues near and far. We borrow the notion of "uncreativity" from Kenneth Goldsmith as he develops it in his book *Uncreative Writing* (2011). Goldsmith makes the case that in this historical moment when each of us is bombarded by tens of thousands of words a day, writing consists of a series of decisions. These include selecting information, reappropriating and decontextualizing it, then reframing it to make what is essentially a new text. In a sense, then, the act of writing is "uncreative." This idea does not map well onto the romanticized notion of the lone writer sequestered in a study striving to generate a singularly original idea. Rather, Goldsmith makes the point that writing is a profoundly social act. The texts we generate are an amalgam of all the texts we encounter every day—the poetry read in English class, the posts we read and write on social networking sites, the text messages we send and receive, the conversations we overhear and the ones we participate in. Writers select from all of these texts those that resonate, then remix them to generate "new" texts that are essentially mash-ups of the old.

When extended to teaching, uncreativity is an exciting and even a comforting prospect, because it means that when we design instruction we don't have to start from scratch. In fact, doing so would foreclose the chance to "stand on the shoulders of giants," to borrow a phrase attributed to Sir Isaac Newton in 1676 (see Turnbull, 2008). In this case, those giants would be the wise, experienced, grounded educators whose mindsets and practices we admire. Goldsmith's term acknowledges that we rarely develop a completely new strategy of our own accord. Rather, we most often select and remix other practices that we've read about or used previously that are consonant with our guiding poses, adapting them as necessary for a new context. Cindy refers to this process as "professional thievery" with her preservice teachers and heartily recommends that they commit it.

Hacking can also involve wholesale critique, challenge, and reconceptualization of seemingly immutable constraints, such as the literary canon, which we'll discuss at length in Chapter 5. When you engage in this more radical form of hacking, it's essential that you are standing firm in the teaching poses you embrace, as these are grounded in a sound body of theory and research such as we've referenced in this book. Admittedly, wholesale hacking can be a challenge, especially when you are required to abide by routine systemic constraints that challenge those very poses and the teaching practices that issue from them.

This is especially true in today's political climate, where strictures on education have reached their zenith. Yet it's important to remember that even before the standards and accountability movement, curriculum constraints have existed in the form of district rules, book budgets, required writing assignments like the research paper, and assigned textbooks. Nevertheless, we know from personal experience that it is still possible to be innovative within these constraints.

For instance, when Cindy taught British Literature to 12th-graders, she was required to use a behemoth anthology with tissue-thin pages and texts arranged in chronological order. There was no way that students could read every included text, and if she assigned "Beowulf" and proceeded by assigning every text in chronological order, the possibility of reaching the 20th century was slim to none. So rather than marching students through the book text by text, she hacked the expectation by grouping texts together around themes students would find meaningful. She supplemented the selections from the textbook with texts from other time periods and multiple genres, including film, art, photography, music, and video. She incorporated nonfiction texts and texts written by authors from a range of backgrounds and cultures. Students generated their own questions related to the unit themes and used these questions as lenses through which to view the texts they were reading and also as prompts for generating their own texts. This inquiry-oriented approach increased the chances for student buy-in and positioned them as constructors of their own knowledge rather than recipients of someone else's. They became participants in an ongoing conversation about themes relevant to the human experience by transacting with existing texts and constructing their own.

At this writing, the requirement to teach from assigned textbooks pales in comparison to an even larger constraint that is ripe for hacking: the Common Core State Standards (CCSS) (NGACBP & CCSSO, 2010). Because they have become a political lightning rod of late, largely connected to concerns about federal overreach in education (see Johnson, 2015), the fate of the CCSS remains to be seen. We are confident, however, that explicit expectations for what students should know and be able to do in the discipline of English Language Arts will remain, whether these are referred to as standards, objectives, learning outcomes, or some other term du jour.

Thus, sticking our heads in the ground as teachers and pretending the standards do not exist, while perhaps tempting, is an impractical reaction if we want to remain in the classroom. If you take the stance that standards are "hackable" like we have, however, we suspect you will discover that considerable liberty exists in determining how they might be enacted. As support for this subversive rationale, consider this statement from CCSS Appendix A regarding the selection of appropriate classroom texts to include in one's curriculum: "Such assessments are best made by teachers employing their professional judgment, experience, and knowledge of their students and the subject" (p. 4).

Hmm. In that case, let us interpret "professional judgment" to mean hacking. Let us keep our students' needs, our teaching contexts, and our own personal standards foremost in mind. Let us recognize the omissions in the standards and address them anyway. Let us exercise our capacity for uncreative teaching by developing curriculum that meets the standards in unexpected ways.

HACKING *HAMLET*

Cindy and high school English teacher Jenny St. Romain heeded these exhortations when they team-taught *Hamlet* to Jenny's students, all seniors, in her Advanced Placement (AP) Literature class. In addition to the CCSS, another factor that constrained Jenny's teaching was the requirement that she teach a Shakespearean play. She was also bound by the course expectations for AP Literature, especially since students would be required to write timed analytical essays for the AP exam they would be taking in a few weeks. Rather than tackling all of these constraints through traditional instruction, such as teacher-centered discussion, round-robin reading of the play, and highly structured essays, Jenny and Cindy decided to "hack *Hamlet*" instead.

While these constraints hovered in the back of Jenny and Cindy's minds, they weren't the starting point for their unit design. Rather, the following questions were at the forefront of their thinking as they planned and taught the unit:

- What did Jenny's students need, emotionally and intellectually, in this, their last high school English class? What essential questions, challenges, and concerns were they currently facing or would they be likely to face as they moved on to college and ultimately into the rest of their lives?

- How did these questions and challenges intersect with those experienced by Hamlet and other characters in the play?
- What were some other texts that students could read, view, and listen to that would simultaneously address these concerns and offer perspectives beyond those present in *Hamlet*?
- What texts would students produce to demonstrate their provisional understanding of the unit's essential questions as illuminated by the texts they had read, viewed, and heard?

Mulling over these questions in the context of *Hamlet*, Jenny and Cindy concluded that the play wasn't as far removed from the students' world as it might appear at first glance. Like Hamlet, Jenny's students were intimately acquainted with existential questions at this point in their lives: *Who am I? How is my identity shaped by my circumstances and relationships? How do I claim it as my own? Who can I trust? Where am I headed?* Although Hamlet is often played as an adult in stage and film renditions of the play, he has much in common with contemporary youth. His father is absent and his mother is preoccupied with her own relationship, one with his uncle, no less. His relationship with his girlfriend is on the rocks, largely because her father and brother suspect that Hamlet is up to no good. His friends have the deepest knowledge of his emotional struggles, but even some of them are disloyal.

Jenny confirmed that her students would find Hamlet's circumstances familiar, though like most contemporary readers, they would probably find Shakespeare's Elizabethan English to be distancing. To mitigate these challenges, she and Cindy determined that organizing the unit around a resonant theme would help students establish immediate connections to the text. In discussing the play, they agreed that the most famous line is "To be or not to be? That is the question." Everyone's answer, including Hamlet's, has to do with how resilient they view themselves to be. Therein lay the unit theme: resiliency.

Having chosen a theme rooted in students' emotional needs and immediate concerns, Jenny and Cindy next selected texts and designed culminating assessments that would simultaneously engage students and meet curricular constraints, including addressing standards and preparing students for the upcoming AP exam. They agreed that although *Hamlet* would anchor the unit, they also wanted to include contemporary and multimodal texts representing diverse voices. Using a unit-planning strategy recommended by Sarah Brown Wessling (2011), they selected three kinds of texts: *fulcrum, context,* and *texture* texts linked by a common theme or question, in this case, resiliency. As Wessling's term suggests, the *fulcrum text* is the anchor, usually a book-length text in a unit—*Hamlet*, for example. They also selected *context texts* (i.e., short, accessible texts) to use at the start of the unit to frame and develop the resiliency theme. These included video interviews with Vietnam veterans who used a tap code to communicate with fellow POWs, StoryCorps vignettes, photographs taken in New York City on 9/11, resiliency quizzes, excerpts of psychology texts, and so forth.

Finally, they compiled a set of *texture texts* (i.e., more demanding, nuanced, structurally complex texts) to teach during and after the play that would highlight its finer points (e.g., Hamlet's shifting goals, character loyalties, etc.) and deepen and refine the students' understanding of resiliency by introducing other writers' perspectives. For instance, students watched Hamlet's "to be or not to be" soliloquy from four different films and considered how directorial decisions and performers' choices shaped the audience's interpretations in each version and supported or challenged their own interpretation of the scene. In tandem with scenes featuring Hamlet and Ophelia, they listened to "Error at First Base," standup comic Mike Birbiglia's podcast from *This American Life* describing his awkward romantic attempts in junior high. When focusing on Hamlet's ambivalent relationship with his father, they viewed African-American slam poet Daniel Beaty's performance of "Knock, Knock," wherein Beaty addresses his own absent father. After the scene where Hamlet's suspicions about his father's murderer are confirmed, they also read "A Dream Deferred" by Langston Hughes, discussing actions available to individuals who have been personally and systemically wronged.

After completing *Hamlet*, students divided into small groups to form book clubs where they read and discussed one of the following texture texts of their choice also centered on the resiliency theme: *Shine* (Myracle, 2011), a novel centered around a hate crime against a young gay man in a small Southern town; *Unbroken: A WWII Story of Survival and Redemption,* on the life of Louis Zamperini (Hillenbrand, 2010); *The Fault in Our Stars* (Green, 2012), a novel focused on the relationship between two teens with cancer; or *The Book Thief* (Zusak, 2007), a novel set in Nazi Germany about a young girl who defiantly steals books and shares them with others.

In terms of culminating assessments, Jenny felt that providing students with opportunities to practice for the AP exam was important, given their heightening anxiety as the test date approached. Yet she and Cindy also knew they wanted to do more than teach to the test. Ultimately, they designed two assessments: 1) a timed essay on an open-ended, AP-like prompt concerning resiliency, and 2) a collaborative book trailer project on the book club books. As for standards, with the CCSS document in hand, Jenny and Cindy highlighted one to two standards in all four categories—reading, writing, speaking and listening, and language—that would be reasonable to address in line with student learning needs and Jenny's curricular decisions and constraints. The standards provided guidance for developing daily instruction and learning activities. Without providing detailed lesson plans for the entire unit, Table 2.2 provides examples of daily activities aligned with selected CCSS anchor standards from all four categories.

Table 2.2. Alignment of Classroom Activities with Common Core Anchor Standards

Category	Sample Daily Activities	Featured Standards
Reading	Analysis of contrasting film clips Reading varied genres and an array of fiction and nonfiction texts around the theme of resiliency	7. Integrate and evaluate content presented in diverse formats and media, including visually and quantitatively, as well as in words. 9. Analyze how two or more texts address similar themes or topics in order to build knowledge or to compare the approaches the authors take
Writing	Timed essay on *Hamlet* Creating book trailers	1. Write arguments to support claims in an analysis of substantive topics or texts, using valid reasoning and relevant and sufficient evidence. 6. Use technology, including the Internet, to produce and publish writing and to interact and collaborate with others.
Speaking and Listening	Book club discussions Listening to Mike Birbiglia podcast	1. Prepare for and participate effectively in a range of conversations and collaborations with diverse partners, building on others' ideas and expressing their own clearly and persuasively. 3. Evaluate a speaker's point of view, reasoning, and use of evidence and rhetoric.
Language	Discussing effectiveness of Daniel Beaty's language choices in "Knock, Knock" Interactive mini-lessons on deciphering archaic language and interpreting inverted lines in *Hamlet*	3. Apply knowledge of language to understand how language functions in different contexts, to make effective choices for meaning or style, and to comprehend more fully when reading or listening. 4. Determine or clarify the meaning of unknown and multiple-meaning words and phrases by using context clues, analyzing meaningful word parts, and consulting general and specialized reference materials, as appropriate.

This table and the linear narrative preceding it obscure the wobbling Jenny and Cindy experienced in their attempt to hack the standards. For example, they questioned, how could they integrate a greater number of diverse voices in unit texts? Were they challenging students' thinking enough, or was this just more school as usual? Acting out Shakespeare is fun, but was it deepening students' understanding of the play? What if students weren't adequately prepared for the AP test? Should they cover more material or go into greater depth with fewer texts? Were they *really* meeting the standards? And why wasn't there ever enough time?

Despite their inability to meet all their lofty goals, along with other familiar challenges like technology restrictions at Jenny's school that blocked web resources and spotty student attendance at times, Jenny and Cindy ultimately felt that they and their students wobbled their way toward moments of flow. The unit theme of resiliency indeed resonated with students, and the questions students generated at the unit's start established buy-in and provided a relevant through-line connecting a Shakespearean play—which students often view as far removed from their daily concerns—to contemporary texts from multiple genres, online resources, and other materials outside *Hamlet*. Students learned strategies for close reading and unlocking difficult language in challenging texts, as well as dabbling in basic staging techniques, poetry writing, and film analysis. Finally, they were engaged by challenging final projects that addressed academic realities like the AP exam, yet also integrated digital literacies in the book trailers.

The unit wasn't as perfectly executed as Jenny and Cindy had envisioned it (units never are), but they, too, had felt engaged by the challenge to hack *Hamlet*. They also wound up with deeper questions, in addition to those listed above, that Jenny, as a teacher committed to social justice, wants to address in future units. In fact, at this writing she is conducting teacher research into an element she felt was largely missing in the resiliency unit and has now moved to the forefront of her practice: *How can she teach her mostly affluent, White students to read and write narratives in ways that confront their own privilege, push back against inequitable systems, and be moved toward social action as a result?* Jenny is wobbling around this touchy question, given that many conservative parents in the community interpret this approach as teaching with a political agenda. Support from like-minded National Writing Project teachers and related professional development have encouraged her curriculum revision efforts as a vehicle for hacking systemic constraints.

In this chapter you have encountered educators who view teaching much as Barthelme views writing, as "not much a matter of choice," but instead "both a response to constraint and a seizing of opportunity" (1997, p. 22). As vulnerable learners themselves, they co-construct with their students a production-centered, inquiry-driven environment oriented toward questions that have consequences for learning within and beyond the classroom. As Danielle Filipiak and Nicole Mirra emphasize, this work moves far beyond "doing school." It is identity work for both students and teachers—hard, but worthwhile, and crucial to shaping a more democratic world.

As such, this passage from *A Hacker Manifesto* (Wark, 2004) describing hackers at large might well refer to the Teacher-as-Hacker pose we have outlined in this chapter:

> Hackers create the possibility of new things entering the world. Not always great things, or even good things, but new things. In art, in science, in philosophy and culture, in any production of knowledge where data can be gathered, where information can be extracted from it, and where in that information new possibilities for the world produced, there are hackers hacking the new out of the old. ("Abstraction" chapter, section 004).

We invite you to hack on.

PROVOCATIONS

1. Think back to a powerful learning experience you have had either inside or outside of school. What made this experience memorable? What did the environment look like and sound like? What did it feel like to be a learner in that space? What inspired your learning? What did you make to demonstrate it? Why does this experience still matter to you as a learner? How could you create similar powerful learning experiences and model vulnerable learning for your students?

2. Using the principles of connected learning as a lens for viewing practice, consider to what extent your students' interests drive their learning. What opportunities have you built in for them to connect with peers and interested adults who can serve as resources for their learning?

3. Expanding the previous question, how are you addressing students' own academic concerns? What products are students making and sharing with others beyond your classroom? How do you co-construct with your students a curriculum around shared concerns that matter to all of you in your local context and to the world at large?

4. What are the constraints of the environment where you are teaching or aspire to teach? How can your curriculum hack those constraints, particularly with an eye toward hacking inequitable systemic conditions within and beyond your school? How can you design learning opportunities that will move your students to critique and to take social action addressing these conditions?

5. Setting aside the academic content standards you are required to address for a moment, what are your own personal standards for teaching? Write them down, post them in a prominent place, and refer to them at least weekly as you plan and reflect on your instruction.

CONNECTIONS

Explore the following resources for further insight into hacking your curriculum:

Ito et al. (2013). Connected Learning: An Agenda for Research and Design (dmlhub.net/publications/connected-learning-agenda-for-research-and-design/)

> Ito et al.'s report outlines the main principles of connected learning, offering several case studies of youth engagement in today's age of participatory culture. Also explore the many webinars about connected learning found at connectedlearning.tv.

Garcia, A. (2014). *Teaching in the Connected Learning Classroom* (dmlhub. net/publications/teaching-connected-learning-classroom/)

> This free ebook offers concrete examples of connected learning enacted within schools across the country.

National Writing Project's Digital Is (digitalis.nwp.org)

> This online hub allows National Writing Project teachers to highlight classroom practices in which they investigate classroom applications of digital literacies. Digital Is fosters robust conversation through resource comments and frequently updated blogs.

Maker Education Initiative (makered.org)

> Get your students and fellow teachers involved in the maker movement.

Standards of the National Council of Teachers of English and the International Reading Association: www.ncte.org/standards/ncte-ira

> Look at other ways to envision standards within your school and classroom.

CHAPTER 3

Literacy as Civic Action
What It Means to Teach for Social Change

Bodies swirl around swiveling chairs and three educators move about the sea of semi-organized chaos. Mark Gomez, Patricia Hanson, and Katie Rainge-Briggs are all teachers and cofounders of the Schools for Community Action, a set of three small public schools located in South Central Los Angeles. And while the three teachers are used to working with 9th-graders on a day-to-day basis, they are presently speaking to a roomful of educators and college students at Colorado State University about civic literacies. Attendees came in expecting to sit passively for an academic lecture only to be quickly repositioned as members of a collective learning community (replete with classroom management activities—"If you can hear my voice, clap two times").

Addressing the crowd, Rainge-Briggs dons her teaching voice: "We're going to ask you to organically form into groups of six to find the QR codes hidden throughout this area." Groups meander and search for QR codes (square bar-code-like images that can be scanned by mobile devices to provide text and URLs) that lead to various informational resources. After jotting down information and discussing these sources, groups are given a task card:

> You are an educator in this local community who has a commitment to social justice and transformative and empowering teaching and learning. Your community is filled with assets, deficits, challenges and opportunities. You want to build towards change. How do you do this?

The how, in this instance, has been predetermined: Groups are to create a 60-second elevator pitch for a structural change or reform for a specific audience—parents, community members, school board members, students, or community partners. In addition to the basic instructions and a tight 10-minute deadline until the presentations begin, the teachers have been given several other guidelines for the project. Some requirements read:

- Provide supporting evidence to build your argument for your school reform design.
- Highlight the value of your reform design for students at your school.
- Reference information found in at least 3 of the QR codes.
- Demonstrate creativity and innovation in your collaborative pitch.

Across these guidelines, the educators have focused on writing as a means toward a purposeful outcome. And at the moment, it is one with which many participants are struggling. Scanning the room, groups appear huddled around papers and digital screens. A timer projected on the screen ticks down the remaining time. Occasionally one of the teachers will provide suggestions:

"You have to understand your audience so that you can pitch your ideas with precision. That's why every group has a targeted audience."

When time is up, Ms. Hanson calls for everyone to reconvene, then each group dutifully addresses its imagined audience with a one-minute timer counting down behind them. First, the audience is school board members. Then it is transformed into students. Then parents. Then community members and local community partners. And though the issues and audiences were selected only minutes earlier, the room is invigorated to conceptualize, compose, and perform a collaborative text that extends beyond the confines of "traditional" academic writing. Through the Gomez, Hanson, and Rainge-Briggs' activity, the participants re-enact an actual classroom activity that these teachers use with their 13- and 14-year-old students in their own Los Angeles school.

We begin this chapter with the vignette above because it highlights an example of civically enacted writing. The activity integrates writing toward a purposeful outcome; the composing that participants (and 9th-graders in the activity's original context) complete is developed concurrently with listening, speaking, collaboration, and research. The writing that these teachers—Gomez, Hanson, and Rainge-Briggs—elicited is grounded in their experiences for more than a decade as grassroots organizers for the educational equity of their students in South Central Los Angeles.

And while the activity utilized technology in meaningful ways—playfully hidden QR codes led to online research and evaluation of news articles, nonprofit organizations' mission statements, and executive summaries of research findings—with a bit of restructuring it is not difficult to imagine achieving similar learning outcomes without having to rely on mobile technology or the occasionally faulty wireless Internet connections these teachers use at their schools. Rather than using QR codes and online research, *any* teacher can capture the same kinds of thinking with printed-out prompts and sample primary and secondary documents.

In demonstrating writing that is intended as a meaningful activity, these educators highlight how a civic pose of writing instruction guides the *kinds* of writing we teach and the *purposes* for it. For instance, the elevator pitch in the opening vignette is not merely a rote exercise; these educators continue to work with the pitch, the research behind it, and the writing surrounding it to *actually* address and connect with the school's community. There is no imaginary audience for writing when there is an inherent, well-defined civic outcome.

For most U.S. adults, "civics" is that one-semester class that's tacked onto their senior year of high school (a course frequently disappearing depending on your state); it's about government and voting and stuff. These traditional notions of civics, however, undermine how vital it is for young people today to be able to interact with and engage in civic dialogue both as students and as adults. *Enacting literacy is a civic action.* We compel, we advocate, we comply through the words we wield. Just as importantly, our civic pathways are stifled if we do not know how to articulate our social needs or are silent (see Ginwright, 2009; Peterson, 1991; Schultz, Hodgin, & Paraiso, 2015). Thus, as you construct learning activities for your classroom, we want to advocate that you maintain a clear understanding of writing as a means of engaging civically with the world beyond the walls of the classroom. The pose described in this chapter offers an explanation of why civics is such a crucial component of our responsibilities as ELA educators and how such pedagogical attentiveness can be addressed.

While the civic world that students engage in is often a digital one, we want to stress that this pose is rooted neither in the opinion that technology is the answer to all educational problems nor the opposing claim that the road to hell is paved with digital tablets. Instead, we recognize that the contexts and the tools of writing have altered and that the ways we use technology have shaped our social practices. These changes redefine the meaning of civic agency in today's world as well as the forms it takes.

LITERACY FOR CIVIC ENGAGEMENT: SUPPORT THE DEVELOPMENT OF CIVIC IDENTITY THROUGH LITERACY INSTRUCTION BY:

➤ grounding standards-aligned curricula within current contexts that invite student perspectives and voice;

➤ acknowledging and working through local, national, and historical contexts of power and identity in the texts and writing activities that are encountered within the classroom;

➤ identifying and acting upon the varied positionalities within the classroom—including yours as the educator; and

➤ tying back the components of ELA instruction to the needs of students with regard to power, social capital, and identity within their own public sphere.

WHY CIVICS IN ELA CLASSROOMS?

Sure, some of our students and colleagues have acknowledged, civics is important, but it isn't a central concern for what happens in *English* classrooms. The prevailing assumption is that civics education should be relegated to social studies classes (or even to that one senior-oriented history class). However, the "stuff" of civics is entirely grounded in synthesizing nuanced information from multiple sources and perspectives within the specific localized context where it originated.

For instance, a local and contentious topic salient to us today as we write this in northern Colorado is fracking and its effects on homes, businesses, public spaces, the state's economy, and the environment. Civic engagement around whether or not fracking is a reasonable response to meeting energy demands isn't a simple matter of voting or understanding land-use regulations. We must also acknowledge that a large population of the students we teach may not even be legally allowed to engage civically if civics is defined in such narrow terms. Instead, civic engagement is being able to understand and sort through competing perspectives—in this case on fracking issues—and then to participate in localized discourse to determine the appropriate actions the community should take.

Peeling away the bark of jargon, we find that the pith of civic engagement is having the individual power to understand and take action in areas of personal and social concern that affect one's life and the lives of others in the community and in the broader world. Our definition is fluid and extends far beyond attending a city council meeting or participating in a local demonstration. Instead, advocating, networking, and publishing are all examples of how civic engagement can include a diverse populace, even students under the age of 18, regardless of their primary language or citizenship status.

In their 2004 article "What Kind of Citizen? The Politics of Educating for Democracy," Joel Westheimer and Joseph Kahne identify three forms of citizenship that are typically promoted through education programs: personally responsible, participatory, and justice-oriented. These three types of civics education vary widely in terms of participation in public life (see also Westheimer, 2015). And while Westheimer and Kahne outline a personally responsible citizenship education as a more conservative form of engagement and a justice-oriented citizenship education as one that may critically assess issues of inequality and injustice, all of the forms of civic engagement still center on how students will engage in the public sphere. A personally responsible citizen may be more apt to participate in a food drive while a justice-oriented citizen may focus more on the roots of why people in a community are hungry and how to address such local issues. However, what is lacking in Westheimer and Kahne's analysis is an examination of how and why citizens enter the public sphere, how they formulate their involvement, and how students in particular circumnavigate the distance between the school sphere and the public sphere.

A local debate about what material should be incorporated in the curriculum in an AP history class, for example, elicits varying perspectives and must take into account the location, time, and *culture* in which the debate occurs. Such was the case in the fall of 2014 when dozens of students walked out of Evergreen High School in Colorado to protest a Jefferson County school board member's proposal to create a panel that would review the AP U.S. history curriculum and avoid topics of "civil disorder" (Paul, 2014). These high school students interpreted the proposal as an attempt to censor U.S. history, as undemocratic in nature, and as a violation of their right to a robust education, and they acted upon their convictions. Looking at how texts were synthesized, discussed, and produced as a part of the actions taken by the youth in Jefferson County makes clear the central role literacy plays vis-à-vis one's civic identity.

We contend that similar opportunities to dialogue, question, and wrestle with civic initiatives should be abundant in ELA classrooms at all grade levels. Such activities are easily aligned with academic standards for argumentative writing, text analysis, and language use, as well as standards like this one from the Common Core State Standards for Speaking and Listening: *Prepare for and participate effectively in a range of conversations and collaborations with diverse partners, building on others' ideas and expressing their own clearly and persuasively.* More importantly, however, these experiences provide meaningful and relevant applications for students' literacy skills in ways that matter inside and beyond the classroom.

THE CONTEXT OF TEACHING WRITING CIVICALLY

From a sociocultural perspective on literacy, all writing is communicative in nature; there is a purposeful element for why we compose and for whom (Gee, 2012). Educators committed to exploring a civic pose with respect to writing begin by considering how their classroom activities are purposefully oriented. When crafting an assessment of student analytical skills, can a five-paragraph essay function as an in-the-moment tool for civic action? What if, instead, students were challenged to compose a policy analysis of a local issue? Though much of this chapter looks at the contexts of civics in the 21st century, we want to begin with an explanation of how this work aligns with the interests of ELA educators and to provide guidelines for contextualizing civic writing within the political moment.

- *Persuasion is audience-specific.* The ELA standards being evaluated on today's summative assessments increasingly value persuasive, argumentative writing. Thus, when teaching rhetorical tools of argumentation, a *real-world* audience allows for engaged learning. Issues students can address range from local electoral politics to school-based frustrations to global challenges that students will come to inherit. When we place the stakes of argumentation on *actual* experiences of youth, we negotiate the direction, will, and intent of writing in classrooms.

- **Students must be able to see how their voices effect change.** While it is important for students to have a stake in the civic issues being addressed for composition, ultimately their voices need to be validated. As teachers cannot control the outcome of students' civic involvement beyond the classroom, what *change* looks like is uncertain; so is the tenor of an outcome or the responses from others. This does not mean celebrating false victories on issues students focus on but rather acknowledging the efforts they make. As in national political elections, not all issues go the way one votes or advocates. However, if students are preparing presentations (as in the elevator pitches in the opening vignette), they should be provided the opportunity to actually deliver them to an audience that has a stake in the civic issue at hand. Be this a press conference held after school, a private meeting with a principal, or a Skyped conversation with a representative from a local assembly, such work must not merely be a "show-and-tell" delivery but a genuine exchange with an expected outcome stated to the audience.

- **Student positionality and power need to be delineated and located.** The world is inequitable. Students know this inherently, regardless of the kinds of democratic values one may instill within a classroom. Looking at local data, census reports, income distribution in a city, and qualitative data or *testimonios* can help students name and identify their own cultural positionality—the ways one's race, class, gender, sexuality, and general public performance (Goffman, 1959) combine to affect how their voice is heard by others. As a key step in developing civic power, students must likewise be able to understand from what position their audience is *hearing*, *reading*, and *interpreting* the texts they are writing and sharing.

- **Above all else, context should drive content.** The issues that may foster conversation and civic writing in Patricia's, Katie's, and Mark's classrooms in South Central Los Angeles will likely be very different from the issues that affect classroom life for students in Fort Collins, Colorado. Educators who promote civic writing must keep a vigilant eye on the issues that might incite students toward social action. Likewise, they must foster a classroom environment where students feel challenged, but safe to voice divergent opinions and bring forward new civic topics for consideration and critique.

Ultimately all of these guidelines emphasize the need for blurring the boundaries between school life and public life. In his 1938 monograph, *Experience and Education*, John Dewey challenges "progressive" educators to connect civic experiences in classrooms to those that lie beyond the walls of the school. This very real boundary between *school* engagement and *social* engagement is one that Dewey tangled with across his career. Forty years prior to *Experience and Education*, Dewey was also expressing his frustration about the divide between "School and Society" (1897), and it is telling that more than one hundred years later, we continue to struggle with this as a national issue. As educators, how are we creating generative space for dialogue that persists outside of the 8-to-3 time frame of the school day?

Civics doesn't take a summer vacation, and local politics don't simply occur when mayoral and city council elections roll around. Thus, civics must be a constant and persistent thread throughout education, especially because schools are charged with preparing students to participate in our democracy. Referring to a "growing interchange" in society, Dewey reminds us that "[the] radical reason that the present school cannot organize itself as a natural social unit is because just this element of common and productive activity is absent" (1897, p. 10). In this sense, what is the "common and productive activity" that is seeded within *your* classroom? Taking a civics education pose in the ELA classroom demands focusing writing tasks and production purposefully *"toward justice,"* to invoke a key phrase from a 1965 Martin Luther King speech.

While society has moved into a hyper-connected and "flattened" world (Friedman, 2007), the pace of schools is not only behind, but is behind by entire generations. Educators taking on this pose should take note that our outdated model of schooling presents an opportunity for student civic action. By considering the contexts of schooling, closely reading public policies, examining school histories (nationally and locally), and collecting research data, students in our classrooms can closely align their interest in and disdain for schooling alike to find opportunities for civic engagement.

When teaching high school, Antero achieved flow through leveraging school archives of yearbooks so students could look at the changing demographics of schools. By flipping through the faces of students in the early 1900s and noticing the racial disparities of their communities today, they saw the faces of the school slowly shift from entirely White to predominantly Black and Brown. This simple exercise serves as a reminder that easily accessed materials at a school can function as data for explaining complex areas of civic education. Such an activity models the critical, civic work of educators like Paulo Freire. In his work with illiterate adults in South America, Freire (1970) did not make civic and critical education ancillary to the development of adult literacy practices. Instead, he instilled a "critical consciousness"—conscientization or *conscientização*—in these students as a compulsory component of literacy development.

Freire's insistence on the democratic purpose of education required a hard look at the power dynamics within society. As Freire looked at how verbs were conjugated, he also guided a critical discourse regarding the relationships between social classes through a method that hinged on culture circles (see Finn, 2009; Freire, 1994). The contexts of democratic schooling and ELA instruction in our schools and classrooms, too, will require making clear the power dynamics of our students' communities. As we describe below, the role of anger and of engendering a sense of solidarity with student anger toward social injustice is crucial.

ESTABLISHING A PARTICIPATORY CULTURE OF CIVIC WRITING

In today's digital age, the very sense of what and *where* we consider "public" spaces is being challenged. This is an asset for educators. Digital tools like Skype allow us to bring in guests from the far-flung corners of the earth for civics lessons, debates, and presentations. It is not difficult to highlight for youth that writing is a means of enacting civic agency and sharing one's voice. Even with shifts in technology, the purposes of literacy are still tied to building on, changing with, and addressing the needs and concerns emanating from the social contexts where students live and interact.

In Chapter 2, we highlighted how writing is no longer tethered to production with paper and pencils, but more broadly involves the "making" of artifacts. Civic engagement is also moving into digital spaces in today's always-on culture. As our social interactions extend beyond physical spaces to virtual realms, civic engagement can also be enacted in various online spaces. Different yet interconnected theories of learning and engagement are challenging educators to consider why the instruction in our classrooms must change to meet the new civic landscape of a digital world. In particular, participatory culture extends how we communicate and produce and can lead students toward both powerful and tempered notions of civic engagement as a result.

An understanding of how the civic world is different today begins with an understanding of participatory culture. Henry Jenkins et al. (2009) write, "Participatory culture is emerging as the culture absorbs and responds to the explosion of new media technologies that make it possible for average consumers to archive, annotate, appropriate, and recirculate media content in powerful new ways" (p. 9). And while Jenkins and his colleagues suggest that participatory culture is "emerging," his own research has been documenting participatory culture from engagement in network television (1992) to iconic imagery like Disney characters and horror films (2006) to shifts in how network television has become more participatory. Our own viewing habits, for instance, have highlighted how Twitter hashtags and fan comments have crept into evening news broadcasts, reality television, and holiday specials.

Our participatory culture is likewise evident in the ways youth today "share," "like," and craft content in digital environments for the diverse audiences for whom their ideas and messages are shared and amplified. As Jenkins et al. (2009) have noted, such interactions shift "the focus of literacy from individual expression to community involvement" (p. xiii). Though civic literacy is not the heart of participatory culture research, we want to emphasize the civic opportunities for real-world engagement that exist vis-à-vis this lens for understanding youth engagement. What's more, participatory culture is closely linked to the concept of connected learning discussed in Chapter 2. As we described there, connected learning in informal spaces enables youth to enact informal learning practices that are robust in scope and adaptability. Our own work has highlighted how participatory culture and connected learning can also promote powerful in-school connected learning (Garcia, 2014; O'Donnell-Allen, 2014).

We should note that there has been ongoing consternation among parents, teachers, and news pundits regarding the ways technology can create a passive sense of civic engagement. The idea of "slacktivism" of "clicktivists" is often pointed to in this regard (Gladwell, 2010; Morozov, 2011). In this context, digitally connected millennials are lambasted for lazy notions of civic diligence and action as little more than *liking*, *retweeting*, or—occasionally—commenting on the civically encultured world. However, these assumptions are being challenged by powerful research about what engagement looks like or *can* look like in a digital context. Jenkins, Ford, and Green (2013), for example, highlight how these new digital platforms amplify the voices and actions of civically engaged youth, and argue that clicktivism *can* be legitimated as a form of political participation. Further, texts in classrooms can be seen as portals for online civic discourse. As examples, Young Adult author John Green's organization of "nerdfighters" (Pfister, 2014), and avid J. K. Rowling readers' organization of the Harry Potter Alliance (Kligler-Vilenchik, 2013) highlight how youth today can utilize their own connected learning interests for online civic engagement with quantitatively measurable impacts. We describe below how the myriad cultural and technological changes we've seen in recent years affect writing civically within classrooms and how writing instruction transpires and grows.

Already there is a plethora of research on how digital technology, video games, and social networking can help support new forms of civic engagement (see Kahne, Lee, & Feezell, 2012; Kahne, Middaugh, & Evans, 2008). In a white paper, "Service and Activism in the Digital Age: Supporting Youth Engagement in Public Life," Middaugh et al. (2012) identify four key principles regarding how participatory media can foster civic engagement:

1. Building community and connecting to social movements
2. Encouraging and amplifying youth voice
3. Learning through models and authentic practice
4. Grappling with issues of social justice and fairness

In light of the many ways youth are connected beyond peer networks in schools and at home, civic engagement is much more than what we might traditionally consider as organizing and activism (though these activities, too, continue to be powerful forms of action). Just recently, everything from online boycotts like those we saw in 2012 as thousands of websites—including Wikipedia—blacked out in protest of the Stop Internet Piracy Act, to live-streaming video coverage of protests in Ferguson, Missouri, in 2014 after the slaying of Michael Brown and the non-indictment decision four months later, provide compelling examples of how writing can take place in digital spaces for civic purposes. As Middaugh et al. note, "Civic educators must now not only consider how youth might use digital tools and practices in service of civic and political activity, but how online life is a context for civic and political activity" (2012).

Considering how youth are engaging, building, and communicating in a participatory and connected world today, we must realize why civic writing is not at the forefront of what presently happens in classrooms. Research by danah boyd (2014) highlights how the social lives of teens in today's "networked," participatory culture are often misread or ignored by adults. boyd argues that digital tools "like Facebook and Twitter are providing teens with new opportunities to participate in public life, and this, more than anything else, is what concerns many anxious adults" (p. 10). Aptly, as a book focused on the social lives of today's teens, boyd's monograph about this research is titled *It's Complicated*. And so, recognizing the complicated entanglement of youth socializing, participatory culture, and opportunities for civic engagement, we offer below several ways to shape a personalized pose for civic writing in today's classrooms.

Engaging in participatory politics in classrooms, however, is not simply a choice about looking at online movements or inviting student voices to participate in debates that can be accessed digitally. As we write this, there is a nationwide movement toward one-to-one device programs in many schools that attempts to address inequality of access to digital tools. More students than ever before are accessing the Internet at home or in public spaces like libraries, addressing a "participation gap" (Jenkins, 2008) that has plagued Western society even as other developing nations continue to struggle with a digital divide. Likewise, the U.S. government is pushing to get every U.S. school broadband Internet access over the next decade as part of *The National Broadband Plan* (Federal Communications Commission, 2010).

But are these efforts enough? While access to online content can open up classrooms for civic education, they do not yield transformative learning on their own. In fact, even in the wealth of media-rich classrooms (which are not *all* classrooms today), we can imagine the deficits that are encountered and assumed. In particular, we point to Childers and Post's (1975) definition of *information poverty* as:

a "culture" marked by three characteristics: [1] a low level of processing skills, marked by reading, language, hearing, or eyesight deficiencies; [2] Social isolation in a subculture, leading to unawareness of information known to a larger public, reliance upon rumor and folklore, and dependence on entertainment-oriented media like television; and [3] A tendency to feel fatalistic and helpless, which in turn reduces the likelihood of active information seeking. (quoted in Case, 2007, p. 102)

And though information poverty has clear implications with regard to the digital tools and practices we may bring into our classrooms, it is also tied to the broader discussion of civic literacies at hand throughout this chapter. Considering how students may struggle with fundamental literacies in our classrooms, such as being able to parse and evaluate sources and synthesize complex arguments—the stuff so crucial to today's standards-aligned curriculum—civic writing and dialogue must elevate discourse to be *actionable* and *understandable*. While a plethora of critical research has focused on the former (Dewey, 1916; Fine, 2002), little has been done to support the academic scaffolding specifically needed for civic action in schools.

DOING CIVICS

While we've talked so far about why a pose of civic engagement in ELA writing instruction is necessary and discussed the shifting contexts of civics in the 21st century, we want to offer some very deliberate strategies and examples of what this pose looks like within classrooms. As you take on this pose, there are some fundamental questions to consider in your lesson design process:

- Is your intended lesson one that allows youth to engage critically with the world as they experience it today?
- Is your curriculum framed to invite dialogue and encourage opportunities for dissent?
- Are the expected, assessable outcomes of your instruction applicable to engaging civically? How do you know?

These goals are not simply aspirational, but actionable. In our experiences, teaching civic-minded literacy practices can be embedded in most instructional units. Antero, for example, relied on Mary Shelley's *Frankenstein* to allow students to unpack how society constructs and defines monstrosity. The unit utilized canonical literature to invite students to reflect on constructions of monstrosity that they identified within the South Central Los Angeles community. Pairing the novel with a documentary on a bus hijacking in Rio de Janeiro, *Bus 174* (Padilha, 2002), students were able to scrutinize the actions of the monsters in these texts and how they were seen as such. Applying the conversations that emerged from these two texts, the students then turned an analytic eye to how the graffiti community of Los Angeles was seen by youth, adults, and policymakers. The students developed policy recommendation forms and—in conjunction with the City of Los Angeles Department of Cultural Affairs—were able to share their work publicly.

Students in the class described above were not unified in their positions about graffiti art; some students condemned the illegal work while others sought to highlight the work as a means of necessary self-expression. It is important to recognize that the civic expectations of the unit were not to make the students advocates for or against graffiti art but to allow them to feel that they had a voice that could be heard on the issue. By contacting local media, forwarding their writing to members of the city council, and organizing an informational presentation for their peers, the students were able to speak to various audiences about what graffiti means within their communities.

In another project, Antero's class studied the genre of documentary theater. The students read Luis Valdez's play *Zoot Suit* and Anna Deavere Smith's play *Twilight: Los Angeles, 1992*—a work that uses parts of interviews with individuals who lived through the Los Angeles riots of 1992. Analyzing the conventions of the dramatic genre, the purpose of the content, and the ways these theatrical works challenged dominant expectations of an audience sitting passively while experiencing the performance, students looked at how theater can function as a civic space. These efforts adhered to English–Language Arts Content Standards for California Public Schools (California Department of Education, 1998, the standards instituted at the time), asking students to analyze arguments across primary and secondary sources, to produce multimedia work for specific audiences, and to read closely historical nonfiction and literary fiction for detailed explication; thus, this was not *extra* civic work on top of the ELA requirements of the classroom but a deep integration of civic literacy *within* the curricular framework of the school. In two different years, students from this class then produced and performed their own documentary plays. The first, *A Place at the Table,* found students writing about the experiences of Latino identity within Los Angeles and, in particular, the role that the current and ongoing debate around immigration played on the lives of their families. Featuring several undocumented writers and performers, the play was an emotionally engaging production for viewers and performers alike.

The following year, the class created *Stop It: Our Future, a Threat,* a work that explored how California budget cuts affected students' education. Using Smith's model of word-for-word interviews, the class attempted to document the ideas, questions, and frustrations that the high school community was (and is still) facing in today's economic crisis. These monologues wove together various language practices; various parts of the play were presented in Spanish, Spanglish, African American vernacular, and as a series of text messages. Though some of the grammar occasionally confounded viewers, it reflected the naturally occurring poetry of everyday human speech (and was a topic of ongoing discussion within the class, thus technically aligned with academic standards). Consistent with the focus that this was not a play about indoctrination, the introduction to the play highlighted that this was one snapshot of civic conversation: "This work is offered not as a definitive statement of the effect of the budget cuts in South Central, but as an opportunity to engage in a continuing dialogue with the voices of the present."

These projects all exemplify the idea that a pose focused on civic engagement does not throw out the expectations of the kinds of texts and writing that are encountered in English classrooms. These are standards-aligned projects that coordinate canonical literature and informational texts for civic dialogues.

ADDRESSING POWER AND POSITIONALITY

As we have identified some of the key components of this pose and illustrated what its enactment looks like in classrooms, we need to reiterate a central theme of this book: It is impossible for teachers to exercise political neutrality within the classroom. The title of historian and activist Howard Zinn's (1994) memoir reminds us that *You Can't Be Neutral on a Moving Train*. The wheels of educational reform are constantly in motion, and to move *along* the same route is, in essence, its own political action. As mentioned previously, in our teacher education classes, we often encounter students who resist this notion. Paraphrasing a common argument, we are told that these students *just want to teach* and that the *politics* we discuss are beyond their professional interests and responsibilities. Near the end of this chapter we highlight how controversial civic topics can be addressed within classrooms, but we also know that such work can feel (and in many classroom settings *is*) risky.

At the same time, just as we noted in Chapter 1, culturally proactive teachers must acknowledge the power dynamics within the classroom. The *structures* of schooling are ripe for civic inquiry; thus, teachers must address and allow youth to comfortably question what power looks like within today's classrooms. While we acknowledge that this power is not evenly distributed, we could go a step further in a civic project and look at how this uneven distribution plays out across school and classroom settings: Where in schools and where in cities are students emboldened with more agentive choice? Are such freedoms tied to socioeconomic contexts? How do adults in schools exhibit their *in loco parentis* power in ways that can feel unfair? Such questions are likely to lead to blunt conversations about power. However, students often feel disenfranchised within schools. And if contemporary research in schools is of any indication, this is for good reason (Jocson, 2014; Kozol, 2013; Linton, 2015; Romero et al., 2008; Stovall, 2006).

We thus take the risky position that anger and discontent are important feelings not just to acknowledge, but to foment within classrooms. The struggle for equity that we must engender in youth is a lasting one. In his 2014 NCTE Presidential Address, Ernest Morrell (2015) described this struggle as a beautiful one:

> Think of the struggle as beautiful because you are embracing it. You are embracing a legacy of people who have struggled on behalf of what is right. Unfortunately, in this world we live in, working for what is right will always be a struggle. New teachers, do not wait for that struggle to go away because you will be disheartened. Just pray or

hope that you have the strength to struggle because you are inheriting a legacy of greatness.

Similarly, Claudia Ruitenberg's (2009) description of "political anger" (p. 277) reminds teachers to consider how the withholding of power can elicit frustration or action within a classroom. She describes political anger as:

> the anger or indignation one feels when decisions are made and actions are taken that violate the interpretation and implementation of the ethico-political values of equality and liberty that, one believes, would support a just society. In other words, political anger is aimed at particular configurations of hegemonic social relations.

This anger, in and of itself, is not inherently productive. However, when coupled with the forms of sociocultural learning practices we can foster in classrooms—models of mentorship, apprenticeship, and application of writing within *real-world* contexts—such anger can function as a fulcrum for action.

In her explication of social organizing, Jean Anyon (2009) describes how youth learn ways of civic engagement through peripheral models of participation, and outlines the power that teachers can play in this process. Anyon writes:

> When educators request that students take part in pedagogy involving planning an issue campaign in the local community, in conjunction with others already so engaged . . . they are in effect asking (recruiting) their students into networks, and engaging them in an arena through which they are likely to be asked to participate further. (p. 391)

If such descriptions come as unsurprising, perhaps it is because they mirror the forms of "legitimate peripheral participation" (Lave & Wenger, 1991) that highlight key forms of classroom and out-of-school engagement. It is necessary for us to remind ourselves that critical, civic instruction does not mean eschewing practiced, proven forms of engagement. Instead we must consider how our sound pedagogy pushes on the seams of social disjuncture that our students express and experience daily. We are reminded that our work as teachers of civic engagement "requires the development of a sense of solidarity, and the ability to feel anger on behalf of injustices committed against those in less powerful social positions rather than on behalf of one's own pride" (Ruitenberg, 2009, p. 277).

TACKLING CONTROVERSY WHEN YOU DON'T HAVE TENURE

In the midst of writing this book, we found ourselves continually discussing local issues that were directly affecting the lives of young people in our communities: a summer of social indignation in Ferguson, MO, the AP U.S. History protests and walkouts in nearby Jefferson County, CO, massive testing boycotts from high school youth across the country, and more. Although teachers whom we know felt that students needed to be able to critically discuss and understand these timely issues, they were genuinely concerned with their controversial nature. The question we heard echoed throughout the fall of 2014 was an important one that we paraphrase as follows: *How can I take a meaningful civic education pose without risking getting fired?*

While we offer some context for assuaging these concerns, we also want to assert that such work should, as much as possible, be enacted in collaboration with others. Who are the allies (both in schools and beyond) that can help advocate for the work you are doing in your classroom? Who can work with you when you fear censure and administrative retaliation? Los Angeles Unified School District teacher (and later, president of United Teachers of Los Angeles) Alex Caputo-Pearl illustrated this clearly. Working side by side with parent groups and students in the community where he taught at Crenshaw High School, Caputo-Pearl helped advocate for the needs and educational rights of his community. In 2006, in response to these efforts, the school district transferred Caputo-Pearl against his will. Antero distinctly remembers, during his second year of teaching, carpooling after school with colleagues to the district office to protest the removal of Caputo-Pearl, who was shortly after reinstated (see Goldstein, 2014).

In considering the local and digital allies you can work with in concert, it is important to think about where your pedagogy around civic education aligns with the interests of various groups. These are spaces for reaching flow. Here are some groups to consider:

- Student groups
- Parent organizations
- Local businesses
- Teacher organizations
- Faith-based groups and community agencies (e.g., health clinics, bus riders' union, etc.)
- Local and state government officials

In addition to considering how to build coalitions around the work you may do in your classroom, it is important to be able to reiterate how this work is aligned to standards and local learning objectives. The fact that this work is specifically about being able to meaningfully interpret, produce, share, and voice texts that are contextually grounded is something that cannot be ignored.

Similarly, there is a key difference between deliberate indoctrination within classrooms and being able to support a community of engaged learners in teasing out inequities and contradictions in social life. This is not a pose about guiding youth to regurgitate dogma. Instead teachers must allow *student* voices to guide classroom conversations and facilitate an ongoing dialogue. As a comparison here, consider the validity (and often necessity) in ELA classrooms of teaching portions of the Bible as literature and as a considerable source of literary allusions. The focus of this instruction is not on endorsing the beliefs within this religious text, but of drawing out the contextual meaning from a work that echoes across myriad ELA titles. By the same token, civic education can be understood as deliberately exploring local issues and drawing out meaning in informational texts. The right civic content in a classroom creates buy-in for students and allows them to see literacy as a tool for meaningful action, which in turn helps them develop transferable skills that are assessed on high-stakes tests and expected by university composition instructors and future employers. The literacies fostered in civic-focused ELA classrooms, however, transcend school and career skills, in that they allow students to see that their words and beliefs can transform society.

CONCLUSION

In the aforementioned play *Twilight: Los Angeles, 1992*, Anna Deavere Smith (1994) voices the words of noted chef Alice Waters. Considering a possible impetus for the explosion of violence that occurred on the streets of L.A., she notes:

> The table is a civilizing place. It's where a group comes and they hear points of view, they learn about courtesy and kindness, they learn about what it is to live in a community—live in a family first, but live in a bigger community. That's where it comes from, don't you think?

Particularly as students are engaged in the difficult, often personal conversations about the world of civic action around them and so often denied to them, we are reminded of the dining table that Waters describes. Later in the same interview, Waters continues:

> Do you know that eighty-five percent of kids in this country don't eat one meal with their family a day? I think we just forgot, you know. It just got thrown out that idea of being around a table. And we don't know what got thrown out with it. There are a lot of things that happen around a table; even if you don't *like* what's on the table and

you can't communicate with your family, you have to sit there in a way and wait 'til that guy stops talking so that you go pass the bread to another or use a napkin or a fork or a knife. And those things are becoming very foreign to a lot of children! It's an *offering* to-someone-who-needs-food. It's *healing*. And I think that's what the table is! It's an offering to nourish people!

Literacy, as the lifeblood of civic action, must be at the center of the metaphoric table of our classrooms. We must nourish ourselves and our students with the ability to challenge status quo oppression, to foment change, and to transform society. We need to implicitly *believe* in our students' abilities to change the world; this is the wobble we must constantly address. As teachers taking on a pose that considers the civic imperative of quality literacy instruction, we have important questions to ask ourselves: Where is the place in schools for students to think critically about the world and their relationship to it? If it isn't in your classroom or you're not wobbling with ways to increase spaces for such introspection and action, why not?

We realize that amongst the myriad demands on your instructional time, explicit emphasis on the civic needs of students often languishes. However, as a profession, we need to acknowledge the larger purposes for standards and tests, and the basic function of public education as it exists in the United States today: These mechanisms are either for the equitable distribution of civic identity for young people after they leave our schools, or they are for an unequal distribution. If the former, then the implication is clear that a civic pose is required in our classrooms. Just as important: If you see our educational system as unequally distributing opportunity for students, this implication becomes a mandate for civic lessons, driven by indignation at the social and political inequities that continue to exist in today's world.

PROVOCATIONS

1. This chapter highlighted several prominent national and local issues that students can engage with. What are some of the salient topics that you see emerging within your school and your school's community? What questions could you ask your students in order to unearth some of the civic issues that are important to them that you may not be aware of?

2. Look at the four principles of how participatory media can cultivate civic engagement on page 64. How does your classroom leverage digital tools to provide meaningful opportunities for real world engagement?

3. On page 66, we offer several key questions to guide your classroom outcomes. How can you work these questions into your own construction of standards-aligned curriculum?

4. Civics is often considered the purview of history and social science classes. Are there other teachers in your school you could partner with or collaborate with on key issues? More importantly, are there individuals in your local community who might be willing to work with you?

5. In this chapter we suggested ways to make civics an ELA endeavor, like connecting civic issues to canonical literature and having students produce documentary plays related to local community concerns. What other writing and reading products could you see fitting into your instructional plans?

CONNECTIONS

Explore the following resources for further insight into civic literacy instruction:

Smith, Anna Deavere. (1994). *Twilight: Los Angeles, 1992.*

> Smith's play is an accessible mentor text for classroom instruction that allows students to see ways to produce work that echoes civic voices throughout a community.

Ginwright, Shawn. (2009). *Black Youth Rising: Activism and Radical Healing in Urban America.*

> This book gives a detailed, poignant look at the lives of urban youth of color. Highlighting the voices of this historically marginalized population, Ginwright offers nuanced strategies for engagement and participation.

Ayiti: The Cost of Life—Global Kids & Gamelab (ayiti.globalkids.org/game/)

> This game co-created by students is an Oregon Trail–like look at poverty in Haiti. A game that can be played in a 20-minute period, Ayiti creates rich classroom discussion and is illustrative of the kind of multimodal products youth can create and analyze.

KQED #TeachDoNow (blogs.kqed.org/education/teachdonow/)

> This online "collaborative learning experience" is focused on youth engaging in civic dialogue around contemporary issues. The site can be a space for student engagement with youth nationwide, and also contains numerous resources for classroom instruction.

CHAPTER 4

Embracing Your Inner Writer
What It Means to Teach as a Writer

A lot of people think that writing is about being read. I find that writing
is about knowing what I think and understanding myself better. The fact
that people read what I put on the Internet is secondary to the fact that I
understand now what I was trying to say in a way that I wouldn't have if I
hadn't bothered to write anything down.

—Bud Hunt, educational blogger

Most teachers we know self-identify as readers. We may have fond memories of being read to as a child or of curling up in a favorite chair with a
good book on a rainy afternoon. We are not alone. Try entering the term
"reading" in a Google image search, and you'll find numerous pictures of
smiling children huddled under the covers secretly reading books by flash-
light. The message is that reading is so compelling, children are willing to
risk staying up past bedtime to do it. Another image proclaims the message
that "reading is delicious." Substitute "writing" for "reading" in a Google
search, however, and no parallel images exist. Instead, most images associated with writing reveal students and adults alike in various attitudes of
despair—bodies slumped over keyboards, Calvin (of the *Calvin and Hobbes*
cartoons) wearing his exasperated homework face, writers searching for the
right word with head in hand. Unlike the delicious act of reading, one image shows a frustrated man with a thought bubble over his head that reads,
"Writing is HARD!"

These aren't just idle speculations confirmed in a Google image search.
In "Writing in the 21st Century" (National Council of Teachers of English,
2009), Kathleen Blake Yancey remarks on the privileged place reading holds
in our culture, evidenced by the prominence it holds in the family, church,
and other contexts dear to one's life; the act is at once intimate, social, and
sensory. For many teachers as well, a love for books is what attracted us
to the profession in the first place; we want to inspire the same love in our
students.

When we ask our own students who are studying to become teachers
to reflect on why they chose this career path, they often tell us it is because
books were, and are, essential to their lives. They can't remember a time

when they didn't identify as readers, and they want their future students to do the same. Yet in this chapter we challenge you to add the pose of Teacher as Writer to your teaching identity by taking on the following habits of mind. Doing so is essential not only because it maximizes the learning outcomes of your students, but also because it can be central to your own professional growth.

**TEACHER AS WRITER: DEVELOP AN IDENTITY
AS A WRITER WHO TEACHES AND A TEACHER WHO WRITES BY:**

> ➤ engaging regularly in the practice of writing in order to better understand the rewards and challenges your students will experience as writers;

> ➤ recognizing that assuming a writer identity is essential to educational equity; and

> ➤ joining a community of writers and committing yourself to sustained professional learning in the area of writing instruction.

Admittedly, the Teacher as Writer pose may not feel intuitive at first because as you imagine yourself teaching in your own classroom, you're more likely to see yourself at the front of the room with a book in your hand rather than a writing device. Why is this the case?

Yancey (2009) notes that writing has historically been physically laborious. Her examples include writing on a slate, smudging parchment with ink from a quill pen, or practicing penmanship with a stubby pencil. Perhaps this is why writing has been "associated with unpleasantness—with unsatisfying work and episodes of despair—and thus . . . a good deal of ambivalence" (p. 2). Cindy has observed the same ambivalence among preservice teachers when she teaches a class called "Teaching Composition." Early in the course students complete an assignment wherein they recount memories of learning to write in school and draw on these memories, for better or worse, to imagine the kind of writing teachers they hope to be. Almost every student reveals a checkered past as a writer in school. Although a few remember the standout teacher who encouraged them to write, others remember list after spelling list and grammar exercises that did nothing to improve their writing because they still aren't sure where to place a comma. The majority are still haunted by weeks devoted to test prep and papers bloodied with red ink from the pens of teachers who missed the point of a paper they had really cared about writing. They know they don't want to inflict the same tedium or pain on their own students, but they aren't sure how to meet that goal, and so they wobble mightily around questions such as these: How do they design effective assignments? How do they make writing groups worthwhile? How do they do more than just assign writing, but instead really *teach* students how to write? By the end of the course they usually have some ideas about how to do all these things, but studies continue to show that few teachers—even ELA teachers—are required to complete courses on teaching writing, and thus they feel unprepared to do so (National Commission on Writing, 2003). The common alternative, then, is to default to teaching in the ways they were taught to write. After all, they turned out okay as writers, so won't their students do the same?

Yet many of the recommendations around writing instruction, based on current educational standards and many years of research, have not had a significant impact on students' writing experiences in most schools (National Commission on Writing, 2003). For instance, students still have few opportunities to engage in extended writing beyond a paragraph in length (Applebee & Langer, 2013). Indeed, only a handful of our preservice teachers remember being required to write on a routine basis during school. This perhaps explains the reluctance some of them express when we ask them to meet weekly word-length goals in their blogs or even to quickwrite for 7–10 consecutive minutes during class in response to a prompt related to the topic of study at hand. Even though we ask the class to reflect together on this phenomenon and explain our own rationale as educators for these methods, we can't help but wonder if our students are convinced enough to take up similar methods when they have their own classrooms.

Nevertheless, we keep pressing because we believe that an important step in redressing this omission is to ask preservice teachers to engage in practices aligned with the very same standards they will expect their students to meet. Equally important is supporting new teachers in critiquing time-honored practices that continue to exist, even though research has shown that these have little positive effect on students' writing development (see Hillocks, 1995). Assignments like the five-paragraph essay, for instance, are so common in most of our schooling experiences that it's initially unthinkable not to pass them along to our students. Giving up this and other academic rites of passage can feel downright painful at times (especially if you were really good at writing five-paragraph essays). Shifting practices often requires shifting paradigms, and inevitably entails wobbling.

We dismiss the assumption that teachers don't want to fiddle with theory and research because they're only interested in implementing "best practices" for writing instruction in their classrooms. Assuming that this is the case would only perpetuate the deprofessionalization of teachers by underestimating their capacity to make informed decisions about *why* they do what they do in the classroom (O'Donnell-Allen, 2007). Understanding and *utilizing* theory and research matters for the growth of this profession. Furthermore, theory and practice coexist in a dynamic, dialogic relationship, with the "what" usually coming before the "why." That is, when a practice appears to "work" or doesn't, reflective teachers naturally ask questions and develop theories about why this is the case. Those theories guide subsequent practices, and ideally the cycle continues, even though it takes a substantial amount of time, energy, and commitment to sustain. Teachers don't have to go it alone, but can draw on the knowledge of other theorists and researchers, including teacher researchers, about how to teach in ways that will best support students' learning.

ASSUMING THE POSE OF TEACHER AS WRITER

Of all the identities teachers are expected to assume, being a writer may be the last item on the list. Consider for a moment the time-worn—and we think terribly mistaken—assumption that "those who can't do, teach." Teachers are expected to be readers, confident speakers, and full-fledged members of the grammar police force. But if you apply the same phrase to writing—"those who can't write, teach writing"—others are likely to buy wholeheartedly into the notion, including teachers. Cindy distinctly remembers *the* moment when she challenged this assumption for herself. She was traveling to a conference when the gentleman seated next to her on the plane posed the customary question "What do you do for a living?" Unexpectedly even to herself, she answered, "I'm a writer," even though her day job was definitely teaching high school English. Maybe it was because she had recently published a few feature articles in venues outside of education, but whatever the reason, it was liberating for her to say the phrase out loud: "I am a writer." Admittedly, it felt like a personal risk even though she didn't know a single soul on the plane. But it was the first moment she had intentionally voiced her conviction that "those who teach writing also write."

Of course, not everyone agrees with this assumption. In fact, the discussion of this topic has caused ire in our preservice teaching classes: Students tell us they "get it," but as we mentioned before, when it comes to expecting them to write as part of the class, we get significant pushback. And the debate has been ongoing for years in the English education world. Karen Jost's 1990 letter in *English Journal* titled "Why English Teachers Should Not Write" caused such a stir that an entire forum was devoted to the topic two issues later. In her original article, Jost begins by locating this emphasis on writing in the world of academia: "From the mountain heights of academia a new dictum has been passed [. . .] the dictum is this: writing teachers should write" (p. 65). In describing writing as a "pleasant hobby" and "condition for future employment" for professors, Jost claims that unreasonable expectations are thus placed on K–12 educators.

Responses in the follow-up issue (September 1990) ranged from challenging the assumptions of Jost's comments to offering pragmatic, rewarding models of writing with students in the classroom, such as Christenbury's explanation that "I do write with my students, and, in my opinion, what I do is sufficient. Maybe my low level approach might be more workable than whatever heroic efforts you [Jost] feel 'the academics' have in mind" (p. 30).

Likewise, Krest (1990) describes how her own writing practices affect the way she can describe to students "how to allow their personalities to show through their words" (p. 7). And though Jost's appeal to teachers was largely challenged in the pages of *English Journal*, the editors also published a smattering of letters that applauded Jost's forthright concerns. We want to acknowledge our view that writing isn't always the "pleasant hobby" Jost describes; we further admit that our insistence that our preservice teachers need to be writers may look self-serving (we do after all make our living in the "high mountains of academia"). However, as we note below, this dictate is grounded in research, our own personal experiences as teachers and writers, and our awareness that larger issues of equity are at stake.

ESTABLISHING A PRACTICE OF WRITING

Taking on the pose of Teacher as Writer requires that you do what writers do—that is write, and write often. Establishing your own personal routines around this practice can help you maintain it.

The more we write, the clearer it becomes to us that writing is a practice in the same way that shooting free throws is a practice. To write requires *doing what writers do*. Writers must create routines and habits that help them embody their writing identities. One key aspect of the practice of writing that is often ignored in schools (and that we found difficult to develop in some school settings) is the way atmosphere affects writing practice. Cindy, for example, looks for a cup of a coffee and a quiet place to write, or one with minimal ambient noise. At home, she typically sequesters herself in her study, or she haunts local coffee shops, earbuds in place, scribbling on a notepad or tapping on a keyboard. Antero, on the other hand, is more focused when he writes in spaces by himself. He often has music blaring (to the chagrin of the people who share office walls with him): frenetic bebop, punk rock, obnoxious noisy *stuff*. He slouches on couches or perches above his computer at a standing desk.

As collaborators, then, our respective writing routines demand that we write in separate physical spaces, even though our manuscripts live in a common space online on Google Docs. We meet frequently—digitally and face-to-face—in order to calibrate, outline, and move forward with our entwined projects. We have become attuned to the kinds of writing environments that are conducive for sustaining *and* generating writing ideas. Something as seemingly innocuous as atmosphere—the need for good lighting, for instance—has become inextricable from our identities as writers because it helps us get in the right headspace to "do what we do."

For this reason, we ask you to pause for a moment and consider what makes up an optimal environment for you as a writer and what might be detrimental to your practice:

- Where do you write? What does the environment look like?
- Building from this, how are your senses engaged? What do you hear, smell, feel? (Antero reflects on his college days wanting to be a writer and instead learning how to make an abundance of snacks.)
- What are the factors around you that inhibit you as a writer? When you sit down (or stand up or crawl into a corner) to write, what are the factors that pull you out of focus?
- How are you using technology to effectively compose in this space? How is technology using you? Does your computer chime with reminders? Does your smartphone vibrate reminders and text messages? Is the Internet too great a distraction?

To adopt a Teacher as Writer pose means to commit fully to *being* a writer. If technology is a distraction, remember that there are temporary and systematic ways to turn it off. Plus, your texts and email will still be there in an hour when you're done. If you are of the peckish variety and snacks beckon as soon as your words falter, have them at the ready. It may seem strange to place so much emphasis on your own writer identity in a book focused on your reflective teaching practice. However, the changes that come about within our classrooms and with our students start with ourselves.

It is no coincidence that Patrick Camangian chose "Starting With Self" as the title for his 2010 article on critical caring literacies and autoethnography within classrooms. If we are unable, in Camangian's perspective, to understand the challenges, assumptions, and predispositions that affect our work with students, we are destined to fall into the mire of non-caring pedagogies. Extrapolating from this, we believe that the writing practices we employ with our students in classroom spaces are actually reflections of how we hold ourselves as writers and of the routines we use to support this pose. In this sense, perhaps the biggest question that isn't on the list above is this: *Is writing, for you, a daily ritual?* Take choreographer Twyla Tharp, for instance:

> I begin each day of my life with a ritual: I wake up at 5:30 a.m., put on my workout clothes, my leg warmers, my sweatshirts, and my hat. I walk outside my Manhattan home, hail a taxi, and tell the driver to take me to the Pumping Iron gym at 91st Street and First Avenue, where I work out for two hours. The ritual is not the stretching and the weight training I put my body through each morning at the gym; the ritual is the cab. The moment I tell the driver where to go I have completed the ritual. (in Currey, 2013, pp. 222–223)

In *Daily Rituals: How Artists Work* (2013), editor Mason Currey documents the productive, ritualized lives of more than 150 different artists and writers. It should come as no surprise that there is little in common from one artist to another. What worked for philosopher Soren Kierkegaard (lots of walks!) is strikingly different from what helped Truman Capote work

("'I'm a completely horizontal author,' Capote told *The Paris Review* in 1957. 'I can't think unless I'm lying down'" [p. 126]). *Coffee* is a big factor for many of the artists profiled (as it is for us, too). One aspect that *is* noted across the many examples of artists' routines, however, is the emphasis on consistency. *Every day*, these artists get up and go about their very different processes of production.

Every day.

Some take off weekends, a few don't. But the last word in the book's subtitle, *How Artists Work*, must be emphasized. Writing and *being* a writer is work. Some days it may be so joyful and exuberant that we lose all track of time, and ourselves, in our work. But often that is not the case. One's practice as a writer is developed through one's writing practices. We find that part of adopting a Teacher as Writer pose requires us to assume the work-like ethos of writing every day. It is important for teachers and students alike to realize that labor begets habits, which beget identities in return.

As we mentioned previously, that's why we often require the preservice teachers in our classes to maintain blogs on a weekly basis in spite of their inevitable annoyance about this assignment. Their most frequent complaints are they don't have time to blog, they can't think of ideas, and they don't have anything significant to *say* in such spaces. These are wobbles that will be familiar to many of us as we attempt to take on writing identities as part of this pose. Some of our students acknowledge that they aren't writers and are frustrated by the project. But we remind them that at least part of the rationale for the assignment is *because* they will experience this frustration. We want our students to see themselves as writers, and we know from personal experience that this worthwhile identity is earned through struggle. Writers commit themselves to the routine of squaring off against the blank screen and trusting that the words will come. Carving out the necessary space and time helps writing come more naturally. Establishing your own idiosyncratic routines can help you experience flow with this particular pose.

WHY ASSUMING A WRITER POSE MATTERS FOR EDUCATIONAL EQUITY

Connecting to the previous chapter's focus on writing for civic purpose, we propose that the Teacher as Writer pose is one that civically empowers teachers and students alike. Contrary to Jost's (1990) framing, writing isn't a task reserved for teachers with leisure time and smooth-sailing advanced honors classes. Instead, it is important for all students, but particularly students of color and students in historically marginalized school settings, to *see* their teachers write. Making writing something that is acceptable, encouraged, *expected* of historically marginalized youth is about affecting youth identity and social transformation.

In Antero's experiences with teaching marginalized youth, writing was not something typically embraced in classrooms. The social norms of urban schools characterized writing as something that *other people* did. These interpretations fall predictably in line with the notion of labeling academically successful youth as "acting White," as noted by Fordham and Ogbu (1986). Expanding on and clarifying this research, Ogbu has reframed his work to explain that youth who resist dominant cultural practices take on an "oppositional identity" (1991). Finn (2009) also emphasizes the direct connection between the need for equity and students' writing identities: "Members of the oppressed group come to regard certain beliefs, skills, tastes, values, attitudes, and behaviors as *not* appropriate for them because they are associated with the dominant culture. Adopting these is seen as surrendering to the enemy" (p. 42). Taking this perspective and considering it pedagogically, writing *with* our students inculcates a sense of community and of understanding the existing "language of power" (Delpit, 2006).

Furthermore, it lets students in on the secret that there *is* no secret to being a writer, although the act of writing is often *hard*. When we write with our students we model how to weather wobble—those moments when writing feels strenuous and frustrating. We, too, are reminded that this is the same frustration that our students go through each day in our classrooms, and our resistance mirrors theirs. Many literacy researchers have investigated resistance and identity with regard to writing in schools (Everhart, 1983). Part of what we suspect makes writing so hard in schools isn't just the genre of writing in the dialect of Standard English that many assignments require, or even the fact that teachers may not have offered clear expectations for the writing that they are requiring students to turn in. Rather, we believe the difficulty lies in the fact that no clear picture exists of what *being* a writer looks like or feels like in schools.

There is a romantic image, we suspect, in many students' heads of the individual writer, off in a picturesque cabin clacking away at a beautiful typewriter, hour in and hour out. The image portrays a writer fully immersed in her or his words, content with a steaming cup of joe and pages to fill. Even today, with several books and articles under our individual belts, we still conjure this archetype when we think abstractly of "writing," and we suspect that students share that image. And while several of the artists profiled in Currey (2013) do indeed clock in to their writing spaces each day, generally that's not how the literary sausage is made. Students at 2 a.m. staring at the winking cursor know this. Instructors know this. We *know* that writing is hard and that the hardest part about it is just doing it. It is easy to pay lip service to the value of writing with our students, but actually writing *with* our students visibly addresses their need for a more realistic image they can see right in front of their eyes, while at the same time reinforcing and clarifying this value for adults.

Further, there is a growing body of research and teaching strategies that emphasizes how writing functions as a powerful tool for shaping student identities and attitudes toward social justice. In the previously mentioned article, "Starting with Self: Teaching Autoethnography to Foster Critically Caring Literacies," Camangian (2010) emphasizes how youth writing can engender social consciousness. Likewise, *Writing for Change* (National Writing Project, 2006) positions writing not as an instrument for teaching and communication in classrooms but as a tool for social action that is central to identity. Pleasurable escape? Sure, it would be nice if every single one of our students fell in love with writing just for the pure joy it can bring. Some will. Even those who don't, however, deserve the example of teachers who demonstrate the critical role writing plays in our lives as human beings and as social agents in schools. When both students and teachers are fellow writers operating in a joint "speech community" (Hymes, 1972), the power dynamics are realigned so that classrooms become more democratic spaces that reflect sustainable social futures.

POWER IN NUMBERS

We have found that participating in a community of writers is essential to achieving flow within the Teacher as Writer pose, both for moral support through the previously described struggles writers face and for the cross-fertilization of ideas these communities afford. In relation to creativity and innovation, Western culture prizes the accomplishments of the individual, despite the fact that most celebrated individuals operate within existing domains that depend on the input and support of others (Csikszentmithalyi, 1990; Gardner, 2011; John-Steiner, 2006). Even though we typically picture one painter poised in front of the canvas, one composer puzzling over a score, one scientist holding a beaker to the light, none of them creates in a vacuum. Painters depend on patrons and draw inspiration from artistic circles and popular culture; composers have always practiced remix; the trend for Nobel Prizes in chemistry to be awarded to individuals has reversed in recent years. Whether they acknowledge it publicly or not, creators devise their work in a cultural context (Sawyer, 2012).

Writing is no different.

Our personal commitment to writing in community extends beyond traditional forums for professional development like conferences and district workshops. We both consider Twitter and Facebook to be part of our "professional learning network." As often as we use these tools to post personal updates and pictures of our undeniably fascinating dogs, we also link to education-related websites, re-tweet smart things other literacy researchers and our own students have said, and participate in real-time professional conversations on #engchat about topics like assessment and digital writing. We also write, read, and comment on educators' blogs.

Both of us have shared our work in writing groups over the years, and many of our publications are coauthored. Even though these have historically "counted less" than single-authored publications in the metric our university uses to measure scholarly output, we have argued again and again that this ought not be the case. Writing in community actually takes *more* time, not less. So why do we choose to do it? Because it sharpens our thinking. It improves our final product. It also allows us to speak with authority about the writing process from the inside out. We aren't just the assigners and evaluators of our students' writing; we are their fellow writers. We support and commiserate with our students through the process because we are writing, too. We comment on works in progress on their blogs and posts on class forums, and ask them to do the same for ours. We celebrate the completion of our respective final drafts. In the process, we flatten the teacher-student hierarchy by conversing writer-to-writer and simultaneously demonstrating the value of engaging in the long tradition of participating in a community of writers.

In November 2013, we joined a much larger writing community. Along with more than 200,000 other people, we launched into 30 days of *intense* writing. Though most of the other participants who were writing had volunteered for National Novel Writing Month (or NaNoWriMo for short), we were committed to AcWriMo—a contingent of other academic nerds writing papers and dissertations and presentations. NaNoWriMo challenges people to write 50,000 words in the month of November. It's a staggering number of words, but when broken into daily doses, it amounts to just shy of 1700 words per day and feels (slightly) less daunting.

The NaNoWriMo website (nanowrimo.org) formalizes a social network of online support through a forum, pep-talk letters by professional writers, and announcements of local NaNoWriMo write-ins. What we think is important to share here isn't how awesome it feels to have so much writing completed on projects we are working on. Instead, we are interested in how the practice of writing is supported and fundamentally different in today's digital age. When we write in the morning and add our progress to a growing number of tweets where we share our progress, we join a community of other writers. Technology helps hold us accountable by connecting our own literacy practices with others'.

To be sure, NaNoWriMo privileges quantity over quality. The question at the end of a month of writing *isn't* "Did you write something good?" It is instead, "Did you write the number of words you said you would?" Significant editing and pruning are required to get verbiage from NaNoWriMo into something publicly presentable. You aren't winning Pulitzers with your NaNoWriMo text. You are, however, building a writing *habit* and doing so with a collective. While we took a few days off after the marathon-like process of committing to NaNoWriMo, the 30 days of continual gunning down the blank screen made writing in December that much easier and familiar and even generated initial drafts of some of the materials for this book.

And this brings us to a significant tension: At its heart, what makes NaNoWriMo a *somewhat* sustainable model for us was the fact that we balanced each other's writing as well as that of a community. This writing space during the month of November helped us eliminate excuses in our lives. Unsurprisingly, our email inboxes remained as cluttered as they had been at any other point in the year. Our students were still alive and relatively well attended to. We didn't look like estranged relatives to our family members. Best of all, we were relatively unhampered by writer's block because a friend-driven pact buoyed us toward completing our daily word count. Over the month, both our occasional frustrations and Ray Bradbury's sense of "joy" in writing were shared. As he notes:

> I've never worked a day in my life. The joy of writing has propelled me from day to day and year to year. I want you to envy me, my joy. Get out of here tonight and say: "Am I being joyful?" And if you've got a writer's block, you can cure it this evening by stopping whatever you're writing and doing something else. You picked the wrong subject. (2001)

Moving beyond the excuse of writer's block, we recognize that writing is laborious. (This is why doctoral students never have houses so clean as they do when writing their dissertations.) Yet writing in a community—whether face-to-face or virtually—definitely helps.

Joining a community of teachers who write is equally important to maintaining a Teacher as Writer pose. The National Writing Project (NWP) has been one such community for us. This network connects K-16 teachers in all content areas across the nation, not by offering a set of universal teaching strategies, but by providing professional development experiences and other resources that are rooted in the principle that the best teachers of writing are writers themselves. As a matter of course, teachers participating in NWP professional development programs not only study theory and research on writing pedagogy and learn strategies for teaching writing, but as the NWP website (nwp.org) explains, they also have "frequent and ongoing opportunities . . . to write"—a phrase that echoes the practices that academic standards require students to engage in as well.

The support NWP provides through its many programs can span the entirety of one's career. The organization's model communicates that one doesn't learn to teach writing once and for all; rather, getting better as a writing teacher is best done in the company of others who are committed to deepening their classroom practice through sustained opportunities to write, learn, and lead together.

In our own experiences, these expectations and practices can be at once terrifying and liberating. Yet as a result of their membership in their own writing communities, NWP teachers carve out similar spaces in their classrooms for their students. They open their classroom doors to share their learning with colleagues, and they develop an inquiry stance toward their work. Furthermore, extensive research indicates that the writing practices all teachers participate in in NWP professional development programs (not just those who have been officially inducted into the NWP network) inevitably result in lasting changes to classroom instruction and to their students' motivation and achievement in writing (National Writing Project, 2010).

We describe NWP at length because it has been so essential to achieving flow in our own development as teachers who write and writers who teach writing, but you can find other communities like DS106.us or can even create a writing group with teachers at your school site like Cindy did when she taught high school English. Antero has also met regularly with writing groups online. At a prescheduled time, he and several friends log on to a Google Hangout and turn off the speakers by "muting" themselves (no one can hear them if they talk or pick up background noise) while they write for 30-45 minutes at a time. The process provides community and accountability, even when they are all writing from homes and coffee shops thousands of miles away. Whether you join a national network like NWP or form a writing group with the teachers down the hall, participating in a community with other writing teachers can play a significant role in your personal and professional growth as a teacher and a writer.

CONCLUSION: SO, YOU'RE A WRITER. NOW WHAT?

In this chapter we have described how the pose of Teacher as Writer can translate into powerful, critically conscious classroom pedagogy. As you take on the dispositions and practices necessary to *be* a writer, we want to remind you that wobble is part of the package. Yet as should be clear by now, we do not see wobble as a liability. From a Vygotskian perspective (1986), feelings of uncertainty and tension as a learner, while not always comfortable, often signal powerful opportunities for development and growth. As we discussed in Chapter 3, by intentionally moving into spaces of discomfort and unfamiliarity, we become vulnerable learners who are open to the possibility of uncovering new ideas and embodying new identities, like seeing ourselves as teachers *and* writers.

While the Teacher as Writer pose can feel daunting, strategies like finding a conducive atmosphere for writing, developing daily writing routines, and participating in writing and teaching communities can help you move from wobble to flow. We have found this pose to be personally and professionally fulfilling, but we also see it as an imperative rooted in educational equity. The act of writing and its accompanying identity are more than privileges enjoyed by those with time for leisure. Even though writing is often cast aside in the education of historically marginalized student populations, all students—particularly those in academically impoverished school spaces—must be able to see their teachers as writers in order to see themselves as writers. By reframing writing not as mere schoolwork, but as work students do in and on the world, we help them recognize their own agency as learners as well as their civic responsibility to enact social change.

PROVOCATIONS

1. Look back at the list of questions on page 80. How does your own physical space reflect and foster the pose of Teacher as Writer? (If you don't have a personal space for writing yet, create one that reflects the identity you want to develop.)

2. Likewise, to what extent does your classroom space enable students to develop a writing identity?

3. What is the activity that allows writing to become a daily ritual for you? For your students?

4. What networks for writers in your local and online communities can help you and your students sustain your writing practice?

5. Also consider the many networks available for teachers of writing. We've focused on the National Writing Project, but that is only one example. How can you connect with these professional networks to sustain your own writing practice and pedagogy?

CONNECTIONS

Explore the following resources for further insight into creative processes and professional networking:

Csikszentmihalyi, Mihaly. (2008). *Flow: The Psychology of Optimal Experience.*

> The research of Csikszentmihalyi offers clear guidance on how to attain states of "flow" and how such routine practices can improve one's output.

Currey, Mason. (2013). *Daily Rituals: How Artists Work.*

> This book acts as a collection of more than 150 artists' and writers' production practices. In looking *across* the examples, Currey's work offers inspiration and tactical suggestions for readers on how to systematize and solidify consistent writing.

DS106.us

> DS106 is a digital storytelling community and resource. As suggested in its tagline—"Start any time, it never ends. Design it your way."—DS106 offers open-ended ideas for multimodal composition on your own schedule.

The National Writing Project

> With a network of more than 50,000 teachers, the National Writing Project supports teachers as writers and writing instruction for learners across schooling contexts. Their network of sites in every state in the United States has helped insure community-sustaining writing practices for more than 40 years. Visit nwp.org to find your local Writing Project site.

CHAPTER 5

Rethinking Reading
What It Means to Curate the Curriculum

> Some old-school English teachers believe that it's less important for students to be engaged and more important for them to know the story of *To Kill a Mockingbird*. Is knowing the story of *To Kill a Mockingbird* important for cultural literacy? Yes, but would that time be better spent . . . ? There are so many important standards to teach, what if you could hit those standards while they're coming out of their seats with excitement, recognition, and identification with the text over [stressing] cultural literacy?
>
> —Elliott Johnston, second-year high school English teacher in a Title One high school with a diverse student population in rural eastern Colorado

In common parlance, a curator is "one who has the care and superintendence of something; *especially:* one in charge of a museum, zoo, or other place of exhibit" (Merriam-Webster). That's because the word "curate" originates from the Latin word *curare*, which means "to care." When we think about what curators in a museum or an art gallery do as they assemble materials for an exhibit, we see five key components. Caring curators:

- research relevant content on a particular subject they care about;
- select the best of those materials for sharing with others;
- organize the content so it's easily accessible to users;
- contextualize the content for users by annotating it, adding information, providing commentary, evaluating the information's usefulness, and so forth; and
- share their collection with users, sometimes via digital means.

Like Elliott, the early-career teacher whose quote opened this chapter, as ELA teachers all of us wobble around the same questions caring curators face, though our materials are the texts we assign and our "users" are our students: *Out of all the texts we could teach to a given group of students, which texts are best? What combination is the most likely to inspire students into "coming out of their seats with excitement, recognition, and identification"?* Because we know the reading, sharing, and discovering of ideas through traditional and multimodal texts is such a large part of the work we do as ELA educators, this chapter broadens the notions of "text" and "reading" to highlight the wobble teachers face in repositioning themselves as critical curators in their classrooms, schools, and districts. Considering the recent emphasis in national standards and high-stakes tests on informational texts in ELA classrooms and *across* content areas, we present a pose that emphasizes purposeful, critical reading of diverse texts, secondary sources, and modes.

TEACHER AS CURATOR: INCREASE POWERFUL,
CULTURALLY PROACTIVE READING CHOICES WITHIN THE CLASSROOM BY:

➤ disrupting traditional, essentializing, or culturally inaccessible curriculum (sometimes by pushing against the canon);

➤ fostering student choice in reading;

➤ helping students persist through challenges inherent in the act of reading; and

➤ cultivating your own passion for reading.

Although museum curators work in a specialized context, for the rest of us the activities of curation aren't so specialized anymore, but are part of everyday life in today's texting, tweeting, sharing, posting, pinning society. When we forward a link, post and comment on an article in a social network, build a collection of inspirational images on sites like Pinterest, or share book recommendations on websites like goodreads.com, we are actively curating online content for our peers, friends, family, and even unseen readers on the Internet. How might our teaching and our students' engagement with all texts—digital and print—change if we adapted the same mindset of curation and exercised a similar disposition of care in planning our curriculum?

In ELA departments and districts, the process of selecting texts that teachers will teach is so routine that we often forget that it is also deeply political. The books available in your school's bookroom, for example, constrain your students' reading choices in school. Whether or not an 11th-grader reads *The Autobiography of Malcolm X*—a text she conceivably might not pick up on her own—can often depend on whether or not an English department has decided to offer, or *curate*, this textual selection for all 11th-graders to read. Although compiling a list of district-approved texts might seem like objective work for a curriculum committee to perform, viewing the process as an act of curation shines a light on the subjective nature of the task. Districts and schools are active curators of the texts that their students read, a fact that has political importance. Lewin's (1943) notion of "gatekeeping" captures well the politically fraught nature of selecting and disseminating texts within classrooms. As noted by Case (2007), "a gatekeeper is one who controls the flow of information over a channel: shaping, emphasizing, or withholding it" (p. 300).

Recognizing both the digital ease of 21st-century curation and the subjective, critical role teachers can play in blocking or enabling student access to ideas within schools, we look carefully in this chapter at the kinds of texts we must curate for students in order to encourage critical consciousness within classrooms. This is not simply about making a list of the "right" texts to teach in your classroom, but about assembling with care a collection of materials that deliberately reflects your commitment to culturally proactive teaching.

DEFINING TEXT AND THE ACT OF READING IN THE 21st CENTURY

What "counts" as text today? Admittedly, the list goes far beyond what might have been considered valid in schools even 20 years ago. The Common Core State Standards, for instance, clearly offer a more expansive sense of text that includes words on paper, images on digital screens, and messages encoded on other surfaces like canvases, sculptures, and billboards. One of the reading standards requires that students in all grades "*integrate and evaluate content presented in diverse formats and media, including visually and quantitatively, as well as in words.*" Even this directive indicates that teachers are in fact obligated to consider the contexts of students' lives when curating the materials they will read: Words, images, music, and interactive media like games, websites, and social media all qualify as "texts" today. Of course, that's not to discount the vast majority of print-based literary texts as well. As the above standard points out, words count, too.

The field of literacy is indebted to a powerful 1996 publication by the New London Group, a collective of literacy researchers who collaborated to broaden the understanding of literacies. By making the word *literacy* plural, they signaled that traditional conceptions of literacy (i.e., as referring only to the ability to read and write) bore expansion. Nearly 20 years later, their research has continued relevance for the ways today's teachers understand "multiliteracies" and the texts that constitute them. As the New London Group writes, "literacy pedagogy now must account for the burgeoning variety of text forms associated with information and multimedia technologies" (1996, p. 9). Digital literacy scholars point to the New London Group's emphasis on how multimodal texts are becoming more prevalent documents to read and write, yet they sometimes disregard the Group's equally strong argument that literacy pedagogy must "account for the context of our culturally and linguistically diverse and increasingly globalised societies; to account for the multifarious cultures that interrelate and the plurality of texts that circulate" (2000, p. 9).

When educators typically discuss "21st-century" texts, we are often equally tempted to invoke only the technology-driven aspects of the New

London Group's work. Yet taking on a curator's role in this pose also requires *at least* equal emphasis on the cultural and linguistic diversity reflected in the students we teach. Doing so begs the question, do the home languages—the *"Englishes"* (Kirkland, 2010)—that your students speak regularly emerge in classroom discourse and the "plurality of texts" that circulate in your classroom? If not, this is a significant omission. Just as important, considering the diverse environments we are encouraging students to interact in, language diversity must be taught in *every* classroom, including suburban and/or affluent school spaces that do not reflect global demographics. Drawing further on the New London Group's work:

> When learners juxtapose different languages, discourses, styles, and approaches, they gain substantively in metacognitive and metalinguistic abilities and in their ability to reflect critically on complex systems and their interactions. At the same time, the use of diversity in tokenistic ways—by creating ethnic or other culturally differentiated commodities in order to exploit specialized niche markets or by adding festive, ethnic colour to classrooms—must not paper over real conflicts of power and interest. Only by dealing authentically with diversity in a structural and historical sense can we create a new, vigorous, and equitable public realm. (p. 15)

As the dual emphases in the New London Group's work make clear, we can't consider which texts to teach without also considering the students in our classrooms who are reading them.

By extension, then, we must also broaden what counts as "reading." The National Council of Teachers of English provides ample direction in this regard. The NCTE Commission on Reading (1999) defines reading simply as "the complex act of construct[ing] meaning with text," and in their discussion of learning to read, includes such texts as books, of course, but also environmental print (e.g., a stop sign), grocery lists, letters, magazines, newspapers, and digital texts. Likewise, the academic standards created by NCTE and the International Reading Association (1996) include print, oral, and visual communications in their definition of texts and point out that because "nonprint texts are an essential part of students' reading experience . . . , opportunities to study and create visual texts—including narrative and documentary films, television, advertisements, maps, illustrations, multimedia/CD resources, and other graphic displays are also crucial" (p. 20). The NCTE Position Statement on 21st-Century Literacies (2013) further clarifies that reading involves more than decoding print texts. Rather, the process entails the ability to "manage, analyze, and synthesize multiple streams of simultaneous information" and to "critique, analyze, and evaluate multimedia texts." Finally, the NCTE Position Statement on Multimodal Literacies (2005) makes clear that 21st-century reading most often involves more than appraisal of a singular text due to the "intertextuality of communication events that include combinations of print, speech, images, sounds, movement, music, and animation." Educators aren't the only ones who need to broaden our notions of texts, readers, and reading, however, because after their many years of schooling, it's likely that students also associate these terms with narrow definitions centered around school-like literacy activities.

So keeping these three shifts in mind—the ever-changing nature of 21st-century texts, the increasing cultural and linguistic diversity in our classrooms and the world, and a broadened notion of reading—where do teachers start in curating an optimal collection of texts for their students to read? To paraphrase Elliott's wobble from the interview of this chapter, what's a teacher to do—teach *The Absolutely True Diary of a Part-Time Indian* or *To Kill a Mockingbird*? As we'll discuss below, we don't see this as an either/or choice, though we concede that a central and perpetual wobble as a curator is ensuring that your text selections reflect the multiliteracies of our contemporary society.

A guiding principle to remember is that the texts that count in your classroom and in your teaching practice are *the texts that you curate as valuable*. If the ideas and language variety found in tweets, YouTube videos, time-tested literature, auto parts manuals, and historical primary documents are important to the questions you want your students to grapple with, you need to adjust your teaching practice to include and validate these texts. The digital and cultural palimpsests on today's language are blueprints for youth participation beyond our classroom. Reflecting the vibrant language that occurs in the "real world" in the texts you curate enhances students' capacity to effectively read, interpret, and interact in their civic world.

WHAT'S IN YOUR BOOKROOM? TEACHING BEYOND THE CANON

Every semester, without fail, our course on Teaching Reading for preservice teachers brings up the inevitable "Shakespeare conversation." It usually starts when a student hesitantly shares a thought weighing on her mind: "I don't think Shakespeare is all that relevant to students today. Why do we even bother teaching it?" The conversation is pedagogical catnip. The class, as if hearing a battle cry, forms two sides, taking on the ancient feud about the relevance of canonical texts. Arguments about the patriarchal and colonial role of "dead White dudes" and rebuttals about being equipped for the ol' water cooler conversation down the road are lobbed at the opposing side. Some students point out that even though teachers may find it easier to help their students connect with contemporary texts like Young Adult literature, teachers can also help them find the relevance in canonical texts. And while we allow student dialogue to *find* relevance for canonical texts like *Romeo & Juliet*, we also point out the possibilities of "hacking" Shakespearean texts, as Cindy and high school English teacher Jennifer St. Romain did in Chapter 2.

In his high school classroom, Antero utilized myriad Shakespearean texts to intersect with contemporary concerns: Gang-related strife echoed sentiments of the fair Verona; racial conflict and systemic treachery featured in *Othello*; capitalist power and corruption recalled the "charmed life" of Macbeth. As these examples show, determining *how* we teach canonical texts requires that we consider what purpose these texts play within our classrooms and students' worlds outside of school. As part of exploring larger, consciousness-raising questions, both of us curated texts by classic authors like Shakespeare, Hemingway, Shelley (both Mary and Percy), and many others that comprise a traditional English "canon" in our classrooms. We didn't teach these texts in isolation, though, but assigned them alongside student blog posts, Central American poetry, magazine covers, and census data. Our reasoning was (and still is) that, yes, students must leave our classrooms with exposure to the canon, but to simply assign canonical books in order to check off texts that students are *supposed* to read is ludicrous.

The notion that a canon of work defines Western culture has been propagated through publication series like *The Great Books of the Western World*, which presumes to offer a definitive list of what books adults in the United States should be exposed to. However, we know that culture is not a static concept; as our population and our diverse beliefs within it change over time, so too do the works of literature that reflect our interests. The limited book lists prescribed by the traditional canon are controlling mechanisms. In *The Gutenberg Galaxy* (1962/2011), Marshall McLuhan describes the introduction of the printing press as a nationalizing force. For the first time in history, all literate citizens could access the *same* texts in ways that would help reinforce and shape the beliefs and identities of large groups of people.

In much the same way, our ELA practices reinforce and guide specific beliefs about valued texts and reading (Applebee, 1992; Applebee & Langer, 2013). Even as contemporary standards dictate that teachers move beyond the literary to include more informational, nonfiction texts, the works of literature that are taught assume even more prestige. We believe that our role as curators must take priority over historical canonical tradition. We must curate to disrupt. We must intentionally select texts that foreground controversial issues such as race, gender, class, politics, and religion, for negotiating among diverse perspectives is crucial to sustaining a dynamic, vibrant democracy.

With this goal in mind, carefully curated texts provide an ideal vehicle for helping students develop negotiating skills that can transfer beyond the classroom. As Cindy's longitudinal study (2011) of secondary students' independent interactions in book clubs indicates, when students from widely varied contexts are supported by teachers to empathically read and thoughtfully discuss a diverse range of texts centered on thorny issues, their worldviews can be broadened or transformed. This is because of a) the vicarious entry literature provides into the lives of others whose circumstances may differ from their own; b) the potentially affirming effects of seeing themselves represented in characters and circumstances that align with their own; and c) the process of negotiating their personal interpretations of these texts in the company of other students whose views vary from their own. Such changes may be gradual, but can nevertheless have a cumulative impact over time (Thein, Beach, & Parks, 2007).

In Cindy's study, she and the teachers with whom she worked intentionally curated a blend of thematically related contemporary and canonical texts that contained controversial issues, then allowed students to choose which ones they'd like to read in book clubs. In a unit on "challenge and identity" in a sophomore ELA class, some titles included *Cry, the Beloved Country* (Paton, 1951), set in apartheid South Africa; *The Curious Incident of the Dog in the Night-Time* (Haddon, 2004), featuring a narrator with Asperger's syndrome; *In the Time of the Butterflies* (Alvarez, 1995), a work of historical fiction recounting the experiences of three sisters resisting political dictatorship in the Dominican Republic in the 1950s; and *Postcards from No Man's Land* (Chambers, 2004), the story of a young man grappling with his sexual identity, uncovering family secrets, and dealing with the controversies of euthanasia. By moving beyond the canon in this way, this culturally proactive pedagogical decision emphasized the differing perspectives authors have portrayed over time on shared questions with no easy answers.

Yet the likelihood that you will be required to assign many of the same canonical texts you had to read in secondary school, which are probably the same ones your parents read, which are also the same texts students have been required to read for umpteen years, is almost certain. This in spite of the fact that the demographics of our student population have drastically changed. According to Arthur Applebee's classic national study (for an overview, see Applebee, 1992), the ten most frequently taught book-length texts in 1989 in public high schools varied little from those taught in 1964. Listed in order of frequency, the 1989 list included *Romeo and Juliet; Macbeth; Huckleberry Finn; Julius Caesar; The Pearl; To Kill a Mockingbird; The Scarlet Letter; Of Mice and Men; Hamlet;* and *The Great Gatsby.* A more recent study (Stallworth & Gibbons, 2011)—focused on the most frequently taught book-length texts in southeastern states—repeats three titles from that list; *The Great Gatsby, Romeo and Juliet,* and *To Kill a Mockingbird.* The variations were written by males: *The Crucible,* the *Odyssey,* and *Night.*

If the worldview of these and other texts included in a traditionally White-male canon do not reflect your own culturally proactive pedagogy and/or your students' cultural backgrounds, needs, or interests, you have a decision to make as you curate the collection of texts you will teach. Will you be complicit in perpetuating this tradition, or will you push back against common expectations that only canonical texts should be taught? Again, in wobbling around this dilemma, you must remind yourself of the political act all teachers are engaged in when selecting and curating one set of texts over others. Who is to say you need to teach Hemingway, another frequently taught author, with aplomb?

At least some of the time, parents will, that's who. Cindy once found herself cornered in a sidelines conversation at a middle school soccer game with another parent who was bemoaning the fact that her son's high school

English teacher had assigned a contemporary book instead of "all those great books kids should be reading—you know, the same ones we read in school, like Hemingway?" Clearly, the parent assumed that Cindy, as an English professor, would wholeheartedly agree. Yet the truth is that Cindy *hates* Hemingway and often weaseled her way out of teaching him as a result. As a reader she recognizes his syntactical contribution to American literature (all those short sentences, finally!), but she can't stomach the fact that his work reflects an overrepresented, White-male perspective of the world that includes sexist portrayals of women and glorification of all things stereotypically "manly," like war, whiskey, and the running of the bulls.

Our point isn't that you should never teach Hemingway. At some point in time, we all have to teach authors we don't like, especially when constrained by district requirements and the limited choices in your school's bookroom. Seeing yourself as a curator helps address this problem, however, because it encourages you to supplement required texts with other materials around compelling themes, questions, and time periods, and to put them into conversation with one another. This strategy for achieving flow can make the experience bearable and even interesting. To reiterate our larger point, however, it is because our own biases and the cultural milieu in which we teach shape the texts we elect to teach that text selection in our classrooms is a political act. It is a battle fought in popular media, in heated online dialogue with colleagues and friends, and in educational policy at the local, state, and national level.

What choices are made available in your school's bookroom? The answer is one that reflects the politics that govern schooling, and if the booklists mentioned previously are any indication, the answer also likely privileges a perspective dominated primarily by White, Eurocentric, heterosexual male voices. In her poignant Technology, Entertainment, and Design (TED) talk (2009), Nigerian author Chimamanda Ngozi Adichie's points to "the danger of a single story." She recounts her early difficulties as a writer to write outside of the perspective she encountered as a young reader who read a preponderance of American and British books. While she admits to loving those books, she explains that "the unintended consequence was that I did not know that people like me could exist in literature." She insists that "stories matter. Many stories matter," because "the consequence of the single story is this: It robs people of dignity. It makes our recognition of our equal humanity difficult. It emphasizes how we are different rather than how we are similar." Adichie's remarks are especially relevant for teachers because she reminds us that the limited, Western stories typically encountered in classrooms can severely limit our students' assumptions of what is possible in the world.

Putting Adichie's argument about "the danger of a single story" into numerical terms, imagine that the texts included in your curriculum roughly reflected recent demographics of the United States, as follows:

- Half of the texts would be written by women;
- 4 in 10 would be written by people of color;

- 6 in 10 would be written by White people; and
- Of the above texts, about 25% would be written by "invisible minorities" (e.g., LGBT persons, persons with disabilities, and so forth).

If you compare these percentages to the list of texts most frequently taught in high schools today, what does this imbalance subtly convey to students about whose stories and perspectives matter most in schools and in the culture at large?

To expand your students' choices and perspectives, keeping the following heuristic nearby can help you work toward flow as you exercise the pose of Teacher as Curator seeking to assemble a set of texts that reflect culturally proactive teaching:

- What texts are non-negotiable in your practice? Why those texts?
- Whose voices and perspectives are privileged in the texts you teach? Whose are excluded? How might you ensure a greater balance?
- Given the focus of the unit you are currently planning at hand, what texts are most imperative in terms of presenting a *range* of beliefs, ideas, and questions for your students to consider?
- What complementary texts (think author, genre, style, time period) might help augment the learning experiences around any texts you are required to teach?

Above all, remember that because each reading selection pushes out others you might teach, you must be deliberate in curating the texts your students will read.

HELPING STUDENTS BECOME CURATORS OF TEXTS THEMSELVES: THE ROLE OF STUDENT CHOICE IN READING

Cell phones in hand and laptop screens up, students are bombarded practically every waking moment with a vast array of texts, as we've broadly defined them above. They read celebrity tweets and texts from friends. They click through websites and scroll through posts on social networks. They watch movies and browse YouTube videos. Yet because these actions don't really "count" as reading in many students' minds, they allow these texts to wash over them without any critical engagement. Although reading has traditionally been defined as decoding words on paper, if we expand the notions of texts and reading as described in this chapter, one almost doesn't have a choice about whether or not to be a reader in the 21st century. As teachers, we must help students understand their agency as readers to make choices about what they read and to develop and shift stances and practices based on the texts encountered and their purposes for reading them.

To see themselves as readers, students must also have opportunities to make decisions about what they will read. Choice is key to agency, though there is much variation regarding what choice looks like in the ELA classroom. Reading workshop proponents (e.g., Atwell, 2014; Miller, 2009) emphasize independent reading over class reading of common texts and advocate that students should have almost unlimited choice in what they read. By getting to know their students as readers through reading conferences and dialogue journals, workshop teachers are able to make appropriate recommendations that will honor students' preferences and reading levels while supporting and stretching their reading development. On the other end of the spectrum are those who tightly control students' reading choices. Despite its designation as an independent reading program, the Accelerated Reader program, for instance, allows students to read only texts keyed to their reading level as determined on a multiple-choice test. Programs like Great Books and Core Knowledge Curriculum limit choice altogether, focusing instead on teacher-led discussions of texts that the entire class reads, often from a predetermined, mostly canonical list. Others promote a mixed approach to choice by combining independent reading programs with whole-class texts (e.g., Gallagher, 2009), or allowing "managed choice" (Allington, 2007), where students choose what they'd like to read from among a set number of texts, for instance in a book club setting (O'Donnell-Allen, 2006, 2011). In fact, in her book club research Cindy found that the social component of reading with peers often inspired students to "read up" by choosing texts that were ostensibly more difficult than they might have managed on their own.

We recommend a *both/and* approach. If students never get to choose texts, they won't develop an identity as readers who engage with texts they enjoy. (If you disagree, imagine your mutinous response if you were allowed to read only what someone or some reading program told you you could.) At the same time, if we don't introduce students to books they may not find on their own and provide no opportunities for shared reading experiences, we limit their access to others' perspectives and contexts beyond our classroom. Furthermore, we decrease the chance that they will develop a *textual lineage* of "enabling texts" that "[move] beyond a sole cognitive focus, such as skill and strategy development, to include a social, cultural, political, spiritual, or economic focus" (Tatum, 2006, p. 47). Tatum isn't using the term "enabling" here in the pejorative sense of coddling. Rather, he's referring to texts that allow students "in some way to be, do, or think differently as a result of the texts" (Tatum, 2008, p. 13).

Enabling texts extend beyond those that students simply like, to include texts that matter to them profoundly on multiple academic, emotional, social, and cultural levels, both in the immediate instance of reading and beyond. Using the reading histories of African American figures like Frederick Douglass as examples, Tatum argues that enabling texts, when read with teachers' support, can improve students' academic and life outcomes by serving as "soft role models" (p. 48). While his research focuses primarily on African-American male students (see Tatum, 2009), he contends that these benefits extend across racial and ethnic lines. Teachers who see themselves as culturally proactive curators intentionally select enabling texts that will reflect and expand students' identities, thereby helping them develop resilience and acquire cultural capital at the same time.

Given our earlier admonitions to push back against the canon, you might be surprised to learn that both of us regularly and intentionally assigned canonical texts in our classrooms. While we don't believe there is a single list of quintessential classic texts that all educated citizens must read, we also don't pretend that reading some classics doesn't matter. Such a pretense would mean ignoring the existence of Delpit's (1988) codes of power, which we discussed in Chapter 4. Yet as culturally proactive teachers, we do not teach these texts unproblematically. Rather, our goal is to help students develop a critical awareness of the canon as a gatekeeping mechanism by understanding how texts function as cultural artifacts, almost like pieces in "a political power game that is . . . being played, and if they want to be in on that game there are certain games that they too must play" (p. 292).

Actually owning the game pieces helps make this point concrete. Recognizing that many of the students in his urban classroom had read relatively few book-length works (due both to students' lack of interest and to previous teachers' emphasis on anthologies of shorter, abridged selections), Antero stuck to his principle of selecting a range of texts because of the themes and ideas they addressed. However, instead of simply assigning them, he followed the suggestion made by several of his mentors and required his students to buy their own copies of Dover Thrift Classics by Shakespeare, Melville, Thoreau, Austen, and other oft-read authors. Costing $1–2 each, the books were affordable to most students and cheap enough that Antero could comfortably cover the expense for the handful of students who were not able to pay for the books. Owning their books had three effects: 1) it bolstered students' reading identities; 2) it allowed them to develop the important college-ready skill of annotation because they could write directly in their books; and 3) it provided a medium that was often underrepresented in many students' homes. Later in the year, by buying (slightly) more expensive copies of non-Dover texts–*The Autobiography of Malcolm X, The Catcher in the Rye,* and *Literacy with an Attitude*—students built their own libraries of books to draw upon in college. This seemingly small decision on Antero's part furthers the idea that when curated for specific social purposes, any text, canonical or otherwise, can shape students' understanding of themselves as readers in the modern world.

In addition to taking the both/and approach of enabling student choice and expanding their horizons, we have the responsibility to help students understand that they will need strategies to navigate the collection of texts that they and their teachers have assembled to read. Reflecting a critical literacy perspective, Freebody and Luke's (1990) "four resources model of reading" is extremely helpful in this regard because it a) helps students understand the complex and expanded roles readers must take on in today's world; b) emphasizes that reading isn't just a cognitive process, but also a social practice; and c) suggests a set of concrete methods readers can use with any text, be it print-based, digital, visual, or multimodal. In this model, the four roles readers take on correspond with a central question, as follows:

1. As *code breakers*, readers must ask, "How do I crack the code of this text?"
2. As *text participants*, readers must ask, "What does this text mean?
3. As *text users*, readers must ask, "What do I do with this text in this present context?
4. As *text analysts*, readers must ask, "What does this text do to me?"

Although their model initially focused on print-based texts, Luke and Freebody (2003) have since extended it to multimodal texts. Their work is predicated on the idea that texts aren't "ideologically neutral" (p. 57) but are embedded in social contexts and practices and bound up in a reader's identity. Lankshear and Knobel (2004) and Serafini (2012) provide helpful reviews of identities that 21st-century readers (whom Lankshear and Knobel refer to as the digitally "at-home") can assume beyond the roles identified by Luke and Freebody, including navigator, interpreter, designer, interrogator, mediator, and jammer. All of these roles emphasize the reader's agency for *constructing* meaning versus simply decoding meaning inherent in the broad range of texts encountered in the 21st century. Further, Lankshear and Knobel blur the boundaries between text users and text producers, pointing out that due to the highly social nature of literacy practices in today's digital contexts, the digitally "at-home" are constantly (and often simultaneously) decoding, interpreting, producing, distributing, and exchanging texts.

Before students can navigate among these roles intentionally, however, they must recognize that an array of texts is worthy of curation. Popular media and digital texts "count" in today's world. Furthermore, this embarrassment of riches is combined with the reality emphasized by Lankshear and Knobel above that reading has now become a participatory endeavor that requires a seamless blend of literacy processes. To "participate meaningfully, young people [need] to be able to read and write; they [need] to know how to connect their contemporary experiences to a much older tradition . . . and to [fuse] the different ways of learning" (Clinton, Jenkins, & McWilliams, 2013, p. 5). Again, this reality demands that teachers take a *both/and* rather than *either/or* stance in curating traditional print and non-print texts and that they welcome the challenge of "help[ing] young people think more deeply about what it means to be a reader and an author in a world where more and more of us can create and circulate what we create with others" (p. 9).

There are many practical ways to help students see themselves as curators and thus engage more eagerly in the act of reading. One strategy is to give them opportunities to create their own texts in conversation with those they are assigned. When assigning *The Things They Carried* by Tim O'Brien, for instance, high school teacher Becky Rupert hacked well-worn practices like teacher-centered discussions geared toward relaying preconceived interpretations of literary texts that students then memorize and parrot back on an exam (Jenkins & Kelley, 2013). Instead, her students brought the book to life, tweeting in character, composing collaborative poems for the Twitter feed she created for the unit, and writing fan fiction that appropriated and remixed the book. These participatory methods still helped students develop close reading practices, but for the far more engaging purpose of composing digitally in conversation with a print text. The examples above demonstrate that extending the role of curation to students is a way of increasing their agency as readers. Our role as teachers is to help them, understanding that they are not only assembling texts, but discovering their purposes and practices for reading (and composing) as well.

ACCESSING CRITICAL TEXTS: ANXIETY AND FRUSTRATION

As we first discussed in Chapter 1, the lifelong wobble with maintaining critical and cultural proactivity in your classroom extends to all facets of your teaching practice. It is not enough to simply open up the doors (or boot up the search engines) and expect students to automatically grapple with the critical "stuff" of transformative and consciousness-raising instruction. In fact, even though we emphasized the importance of choice in the previous section, you are likely to wobble around determining what constitutes an optimal degree of it. Too many choices can actually discourage student agency; dumping too much information on students is just as problematic as denying access to critical texts.

In looking across information behavior research, Donald Case (2007) offers several lessons. The notions that "more information is not always better" and that "context is central to the transfer of information" (p. 327) are particularly useful as you take on the Teacher as Curator pose. Case outlines various strategies noted within information sciences research. Tuning out the "noise" of too much information, for example, may be an important coping strategy students need to use selectively in classroom settings. The plaguing, blinking cursor that encourages writers to go get a snack or check their email may be a problem of analysis-paralysis: "Ignoring or avoiding information is at times a rational strategy for living and working, especially when it promotes psychological coping" (p. 327). At the same time, information may seem too scarce or too abundant. Sometimes students "do not connect external information to their internal reality because of anxiety, or because they do not see the relevance of it. . . . Much of what we bring to bear on information in creating meaning from it is not only 'outside' of the package . . . but also outside of the information itself: our accumulated personal experiences, including our understanding of the world and of language" (p. 327).

We want to underscore the very distinct ways we are understanding anxiety within information science research and frustration within classrooms. Anxiety arises when users are unable to access the *kind* of information they are seeking, such as lyrics to a song, a sentence from a book in order to cite it properly, or a YouTube video of a historic speech. In other words, the anxiety is not about the content but about the processes of *finding* it. Yet we must help students understand that information-seeking may elicit feelings of anxiety. Echoing Vygotskian principles of sociocultural learning, Kuhlthau (1993) writes, "Anxiety may be an integral part of the information-seeking process resulting from uncertainty and confusion. Uncertainty is a necessary critical element in any process of construction. When the information search process is viewed as a process of construction, uncertainty and anxiety are expected as part of the process" (p. 8).

By contrast, frustration with texts within classrooms is about interpretation, understanding, and relatability. While a plethora of texts may be available to students, being able to adequately understand and find meaningful connections among texts can cause frustration. Quoting a student who compares managing information online to "taking a drink from a fire hydrant" (p. 49), Kajder (2010) points out that teachers must "help students leverage the same stream in smart, intentional ways that advance their thinking" (p. 50). She offers teaching strategies and tools to help students "locate/gather, question/critique, connect, and synthesize" information, including teacher modeling, a website evaluation rubric, and social bookmarking tools that allow users to highlight, comment on, and tag relevant information they find.

Regardless of format (i.e., digital, multimodal, or print), texts can also provoke frustration if students find them too difficult to parse meaning from without teacher-supported scaffolding or, conversely, too easy compared to students' developmental level. Earlier, we mentioned the Accelerated Reader (AR) program that guides student reading into various levels. At Antero's school, many students felt frustrated with reading AR books because the "accessible" choices available to them—while quantitatively within the reading band that students were expected to understand—appeared juvenile. Books filled with exceptionally large print and glossy pictures implied that students were incapable readers. Instead of sparking passion for reading, these books actually inhibited students' motivation because the students felt pandered to and disrespected.

In her 1979 speech at the Second Sex Conference, Audre Lorde (1984) described the role of women "who stand outside the circle" of what society delineates as *normal* (p. 112) and asserted that "the master's tools will never dismantle the master's house." Taking up the challenges of frustrating and anxiety-inducing texts, we must remember that the tools of literacy are taken up for intentionally critical and culturally proactive purposes. If we want students to be passionate, civically engaged, and critically conscious readers, we cannot accept many of the *tools* of literacy that are offered for classroom teachers; we need to sometimes deviate from the text choices our teaching peers and administrations suggest, as well as from the often narrowly construed literacy practices that are expected to accompany them. The ability to comfortably ease *through* (not away from) the anxiety of finding information is a political tool we guide students to wield.

As we wobble around curating texts, we must bear in mind—and help students bear in mind—that anxiety and frustration are inevitable emotions attached to textual access in today's world, in the same way that these emotions are attached to learning. As Kuhlthau notes, "Learning is not a simple, straightforward cognitive process of assimilating new information. Affective experience of uncertainty and confusion complicate the process" (p. 28). Returning to Lorde, she notes later in her speech, "In a world of possibility for us all, our personal visions help lay the groundwork for political action" (p. 112). It is toward such political action that we must guide students if they are to better understand *why* finding texts and expending the effort to read them are such important tasks in today's world.

READING PASSIONATELY

As we've discussed throughout this chapter, your curation of texts should be centered around the critical learning opportunities you expect your students to grapple with. Recognizing and valuing their identities as readers, you can help them read willingly, purposefully, and persistently in light of the challenges and opportunities inherent in this 21st-century context, especially when they see their teachers enacting these practices, too. In the final section of this chapter, however, we have an important question strictly for you: Are you maintaining the passion for reading that may have brought you into the profession in the first place?

When posed to our preservice teachers and to early career teachers we know, this question often elicits looks of disbelief. The very enthusiasm of sharing a love of reading with their students that drew them to the ELA classroom temporarily goes underground as college students. "Who has time to read," they groan, "when we can't even keep up with all the reading we're assigned?" We understand how assigned reading can take precedence over passion. Even though we're on the assigning end as professors, we also have to read (and reread) all the texts we teach in our multiple classes. Time presents a considerable wobble for us, too, but we both find it essential to read beyond duty, to challenge our thinking, fan our curiosity, and inhabit imagined worlds. Although Antero has actually tallied up the number of books he can realistically read in a lifetime (which Cindy finds really depressing), we both read pretty indiscriminately—online, in print, off cereal boxes—and use earbuds to "read in audio"—whatever it takes to feed the beast. For us, reading isn't a guilty pleasure, it's a "gentle madness," to lift the title of Nicholas Basbanes's 1995 book about book collectors.

Teacher Donalyn Miller (2009) views herself as a "book whisperer," intent on wooing her middle school students with the right book. We see ourselves as unabashed "book pushers" who are absolutely persuaded that to convey passionate reading, you—as the role model in the classroom—must continue to be a passionate reader yourself. Go ahead and be selfish about it. The rewards of doing so will help you carve out time in your busy day, even if you have to multitask to work through the wobble around time. Antero listens to books while he's driving. Cindy reads while she works out, propping books and research journals up on the panel of the elliptical machine, or reading digital copies from her cellphone that she's downloaded using free apps like Kindle and Nook.

Maintaining a passionate reading practice will help you re-create similar experiences for your own students; this has implications for how you "assign" reading, too. Strategies *are* important, but it's easy to lose sight of the ultimate goal we mentioned above—to help students curate their own texts and view reading as a non-negotiable practice in their lives rather than an instrumental task that gets them through school. That's why it's important to reflect on your own motivations as a reader by considering such questions as:

- *Values:* Why do I read? What is my relationship to the act of reading?
- *Volition:* What do I choose to read? How do these choices connect to my cultural positionality? How does that positionality implicitly shape the texts I'm drawn to, my purposes for reading them, the ways I read them? How might I expand my identity as a reader by reading beyond the confines that my positionality circumscribes?
- *Purposes and Practices:* How do I read? How do I shift my practices as a reader based on immediate contextual constraints? For instance, what is the attitudinal impact on me when I am assigned a book as compared to when I choose a book? How do I read a prescription label differently from how I read a tax form, a novel, a tweet, my Facebook timeline, or a YouTube video?

We recommend that curation of your personal reading selections ultimately fall along (at least) three lines:

1. *You need to read texts that allow you to feel passionate about continuing to be a reader.* Fiction, nonfiction, poetry, trashy romance novels, or police procedural detective yarns, we don't care: You need to be reading books that you look forward to picking up *daily*. Your identity as a Teacher as Reader is as important as that of Teacher as Writer. Your ability to foster passionate reading identities in your students hinges on it.

2. ***You need to read texts that keep your instruction up-to-date with the community, cultural, and youth-focused contexts of your classroom environment.*** Newspapers, student pop culture like films and music, and online blogging sites all help inform you of the kinds of subtle changes, vocabularies, and interests that are filtering into your classroom. Being constantly aware of every piece of information isn't feasible. However, your sense of which media will resonate with students and which news developments need to be explored in classrooms will become more nuanced over time. *Listening to* and *synthesizing* the needs of your students with pressing issues in the world should be key to your curation, especially considering the civic potential of literacy practices that we emphasized in Chapter 3.

3. ***You need to read (and ideally contribute to) texts that better apprise you of ELA instruction and literacies research.*** Keeping practitioner literature, research journals, online networks, and discussion groups with critical friends on your curation list allows you to ensure that the *ways* you are teaching and curating texts for your students are most appropriate for your teaching context. The suggested resources provided throughout this book, for example, point to myriad journals, monographs, and edited collections that are useful for challenging and improving your pedagogy.

In his foreword to Jack Schneider's (2014) book *From the Ivory Tower to the Schoolhouse*, educational researcher Larry Cuban discusses the seeming paradox that more than half of U.S. schoolteachers hold master's degrees and yet teacher expertise is largely ignored in schools. He writes, "Yet in light of so many teachers exposed to research in their graduate programs, an expanding empirical base for effective programs, and a large population of teachers familiar with the ins-and-outs of research, so little of that knowledge has filtered into classroom practice. Decade after decade, critics have characterized teacher use of research as slim." Cuban's intention here isn't to denounce the poor implementation of research by teachers but to better illustrate how teacher knowledge about classroom pedagogy is underutilized within the current climate of educational policy. Furthermore, we can't emphasize enough that the conduit must run both ways, that is, from the schoolhouse to the ivory tower and back. University researchers and policymakers are sorely in need of the inside knowledge of teacher researchers (Cochran-Smith & Lytle, 1992, 2009) who are intimately connected to the classroom's "everyday" (Rose, 1996).

In light of this recognition, we believe that curating your reading of education research is not simply about consuming texts, including journals, blogs, books, webinars, and podcasts. Instead, you must actively share with your colleagues the texts you love to read for pleasure and those you use to enhance your teaching practice. By adopting the pose of Teacher as Writer that we recommended in the previous chapter, you can also include texts you generate yourself, such as blog posts, tweets on educational topics, and even professional articles. Just as you do in your classroom, you must curate the research you hold to be important to your peers, your administrators, and various chains of critical allies. This isn't *hard* work: Casually slipping in the name and a sentence about a book you've read is easy to do, yet it legitimates the body of work that guides your practice. (Ditto sharing the information in spaces like online social networks.)

CONCLUSION

Whether you embrace the radical sentiments expressed in popular Young Adult novels like *The Hunger Games* (Collins, 2008), find nuanced criticality in the words of Hamlet, or reflect on the statistics offered in a new scholarly report, we encourage you to frame your pose as a curator with culturally proactive teaching in mind. In writing about information literacy and the search process, Peter Morville (2005) describes a utopian future based around the notion of "ambient findability": "a fast emerging world where we can find anyone or anything from anywhere at anytime" (p. 6). Morville readily admits that "we're not there yet," but foresees digital and web-based technologies allowing leaps and bounds toward this utopia.

We're not so sure.

As it stands, it's not difficult to *find* the information you're looking for. However, as information is ever more attainable, we believe that the need for careful, deliberate curation becomes ever more important. Knowing what to search for is as important as knowing how and why to do so, particularly in light of the globalized, *flattened* world (Friedman, 2007) that the New London Group (1996) described when framing a definition of multi-literacies. Simply using technologies and informational literacies in schools is not enough if students are unaware of the need to search for issues of global crisis, local politics around equity, and opportunities for access to resources like universities. Even more importantly, facts, breaking news, and images of the changing multimodal world are useful, but so too are the powerful lessons that are embedded in the expressive texts that form the bedrock of the humanities, like literature, poetry, memoir, and the literary essay. Curation is just as much about not losing sight of the texts that we want students to struggle with—and ultimately fall in love with—as it is about being sensitive to the capricious whims of breaking news.

Ultimately, wobbling with curation entails being an attentive reader: challenging traditional notions of text; staying abreast of educational research; being engaged in the texts that appeal to our students. As Elliott illustrates in this chapter's opening quotation, powerful text curation is emotionally fraught. Even as the "great books" that our students may encounter expand in scope and diversity, it is for us—as educators—to wobble with which ones best augment youth understanding in their present realities.

Provocations

1. How do you use reading, broadly defined, to function in your everyday life? How would your students answer this question? To find out, take your students on an informal "literacy field trip" around the school or some nearby public place and observe activities where people are engaging with texts, broadly defined. To guide your observations, we encourage the use of these questions (adapted from Barton & Hamilton, 2000):

   - What is the physical location and social context where reading is occurring?
   - Who are the people involved?
   - What texts are they using? What are they talking about in relation to the text?
   - What are their apparent goals and expectations for successful participation in the event?

   Reviewing the notes from your field trip, how do your observations (and your students') expand your notion of what counts as reading? What are the implications for your curation of texts? How can you help students interpret, critique, and negotiate among the texts they encounter in their everyday lives?

2. Explore your reading identity using the "Identity Map Reflection" from *Flows of Reading* (Riley, Mehta, & Jenkins, Version 82 of this page, updated 22 February 2013), an interactive digital companion to *Reading in a Participatory Culture* (Jenkins & Kelley, 2013): scalar.usc.edu/anvc/flowsofreading/1_4_ReaderIdentityMap?path=1-motives-for-reading. What did you notice? How does it impact your perception of your reading practices?

3. When you find yourself reading and choosing texts to read, what do you tend to choose? Is it fiction? Nonfiction? A book? A magazine? Try reading texts that go against your typical reading choices, even if you initially feel resistant to them. What do you notice about yourself as a reader when you do so? How can these insights help you within your classroom?

CONNECTIONS

Explore the following resources for further insight into text curation:

Anstey, Michele, and Bull, Geoff. (2006). *Teaching and Learning Multiliteracies: Changing Times, Changing Literacies.*

> Find teaching strategies and resources for planning curriculum using Freebody and Luke's (1990) "four resources model of reading" in this teacher-friendly text.

Brain Pickings (brainpickings.org)

> Maria Popova offers a first-rate example of interdisciplinary curation.

Hutchinson, Ashley. "Connecting, Curating and Changing" (digitalis.nwp. org/resource/5227)

> This resource from a high school English teacher from the Tar River Writing Project shows how she helps students become curators by gathering multimodal sources related to interest-based questions of civic importance.

"Teachers as Readers: Forming Book Groups as Professionals" (www.ncte. org/positions/statements/teachersasreaders)

> Interested in forming a teacher book group? This resource offers clear strategies and rationales for doing so.

CHAPTER 6

Classroom Spaces, Cultures, and Possibilities
What It Means to Be a Designer

In their dialogic text about literacy, Paulo Freire and Donaldo Macedo (1987) write, "Reading the world must precede reading the word" (p. 35). Word order is important in this sentence, but it's often overlooked in literacy discussions because we flip the order to correspond with the book's title: *Literacy: Reading the Word and the World.* However, if we assume the authors' intentionality in both cases, it's important to revisit the sentence. This is because interpreting the "codes of power" in society (Delpit, 1988) requires that individuals must be able to decipher the context and cultural environment in which a particular set of words occurs. The *world*, be it a classroom, a home, a park, a student commute from house to bus to school, must be understood and *read*.

By acknowledging that all words are culturally constructed, we contend that the spaces for learning and creating words must also be constructed.

If the context of learning reinforces power structures that are socially constricting for students, the learning experiences of the students in our classrooms are likely to be equally limiting. And these meanings can be—often are—out of the control of teachers. If a student has had largely negative experiences in classrooms prior to yours, then the school environment, *not you as an individual teacher*, may dictate the relational feelings and experiences that transpire. As an example, in an earlier study (Garcia, 2012), Antero describes experiences with a 9th-grader who came into his classroom in the middle of the year as a transfer student. Upon entering the classroom, the student—known in the study as Dante—seemed to advise Antero to leave him alone, warning that he had made his last teacher cry. He looked into Antero's eyes as he said this. And then he returned his attention to his phone. The statement, though interpreted possibly as a threat, was also a declaration about what the classroom space meant to him. Based on his assumed reading of the classroom, Dante advised a well-intentioned teacher that his efforts were moot within the schooling environment, its oppressive structures, and the ways subjugated bodies have been watched and controlled for decades.

It's no secret that today's classrooms, developed for an industrialized working class, are designed for control. The model of panopticon-like surveillance in classrooms, regardless of the purpose or pedagogy of teachers, is one that creates a dynamic of unequal power. Classrooms are typically filled with rows of students oriented in a single direction and desks that make it difficult for bodies to be positioned comfortably. Such desks are important objects to be *read* as a class. Ira Shor in *Critical Teaching and Everyday Life* (1987) discusses working with his community college students and having them "read" the hard metal, mass-produced products that contort bodies in classrooms. The intent of such rooms can be interpreted by the title of Foucault's 1975 work: *Discipline and Punish*. In it, Foucault asks, "Is it surprising that prisons resemble factories, schools, barracks, hospitals, which all resemble prisons?" (p. 228). The answer, of course, especially for educators in urban spaces, is no. The lessons that are inscribed in the well-trodden hallways, unwelcoming furniture, and physical design of schools are not of an academic education but of a civic one: These are spaces that teach youth what life outside of schools—whether in the prison pipeline or in sub-living-wage jobs—will look and feel like. These lessons *can* be erased vis-à-vis a college education and the opportunities to more fluidly navigate environments of higher education with their lack of bells and bathroom passes, and with unfiltered Wi-Fi. But this, too, means that not all students are privy to these lessons.

On the other end of the spectrum, students who attend more affluent schools are able to thrive in the schooling environment and transfer this familiarity to college and future job opportunities. A 2015 episode of the radio program *This American Life*, "Three Miles," highlights the effects of a program in which a teacher in the Bronx brought her high school students from the poorest congressional district in the country to an elite, $43,000-a-year private institution in a pen-pal-like exchange. As the bus pulled up to the pristine campus, the public school students were taken aback, one student even breaking down in tears. The *differences* in how we school students are striking, surprising, life-changing.

In addition to looking a lot like prisons, classrooms also mimic the spaces and practices of the period of industrialization in the United States. The bells that signal new "shifts" in a student's daily labor regimen are meant to mimic the factory-like work that awaited many students in our nation's past. Further, these functions of schools are by no means found only in the United States. As Paul Willis describes in *Learning to Labor* (1981), schooling and resistance to it are elements of inherent, sociohistoric aspects of control. Willis's book begins with a prophetic statement: "The difficult thing to explain about how middle-class kids get middle-class jobs is why others let them. The difficult thing to explain about how working-class kids get working-class jobs is why they let themselves" (p. 1). The sorting mechanisms of schools aren't reflected simply in curriculum and "tracking" (Oakes, 1986). Instead, they proliferated years before your students walked into your classroom.

Further, for more than a century, educators have looked to technology to better liberate classrooms from the cramped quarters of schools. As Larry Cuban has explored (1986), technology has done little but hold an expensive, elusive carrot in front of schools. Yes, the displays in front of classrooms have gotten a little bit shinier in their decades-long transition from chalk to white to SMART Boards. However, Cuban notes that classroom technology presents a "perennial paradox" wherein new tools simply re-create the same conditions of learning over and over again. While technology can be *neat*, we've deliberately stepped away from looking to it in this chapter for answers to the challenges of classroom practice. Instead, we will address how technology can be incorporated into our understanding of space.

With this push against the static nature of classroom environments, we offer this chapter's pose: Teacher as Designer. In addition to shaping culturally proactive classroom space, this pose considers other *spaces* for sculpting, cultivating, and co-designing optimal environments for your students' learning.

TEACHER AS DESIGNER:
CREATE MORE EQUITABLE LEARNING ENVIRONMENTS BY DESIGNING AND CO-DESIGNING THE PHYSICAL AND CULTURAL SPACES OF OUR PRACTICE THROUGH:

➤ Sustaining a classroom space—both physical and virtual—that reflects the needs, lives, and interests of your learning community;

➤ Building a classroom culture that is safe, welcoming, and democratic;

➤ Improvising subversively when schooling conditions shunt you and your students to spaces that would limit learning and diminish morale; and

➤ Coconstructing spaces with students for civic learning by drawing on community experts and local resources.

Being deliberate about how you configure the space of a classroom is a difficult prospect. It's about much more than simply moving desks around a room and putting posters on walls. Antero learned this the hard way one year. In an attempt to build community within his 9th-grade classroom, he stacked all of the desks, chairs, and other movable furniture in the back of the room on the first day of school. He asked his students—who were slightly terrified of their new high school environment—to design the classroom they wanted to engage within. Standing passively with no other directions from Antero, the students did not immediately set about constructing the classroom utopia of their dreams. Instead, after a bit more prodding, students reluctantly grabbed chairs and desks from the back of the room and dutifully put them in rows facing the classroom's whiteboard.

There, they seemed to imply, *we've moved the furniture the way it's supposed to look. Happy now?* Despite Antero's intent to use classroom design as a democratizing opening activity for the school year, the students ultimately re-created the conditions of schooling with which they were most familiar. This anecdote may suggest that it is futile for educators to push or attempt to change perceptions in classrooms when school designs have persisted unchanged for a century. As we'll share through our own examples, it's true that attempts to rewrite classroom space can flounder. Big-time.

However, while Antero's fumbled attempt to transform classrooms is a failed example of how to change a classroom into a liberatory space for learning—a vivid wobble—we offer it as a way to point out that there are more effective ways to accomplish this goal. Below we look at some ways you can undertake a pose around educational design. We deliberately place this chapter near the end of the book as a synthesis of many of the principles found throughout the book. From models of civic intent to principles of connected learning, intentional design will echo sentiments we've previously explored. However, we want to emphasize that designing in spaces of learning and inquiry should be a *humanizing process* that includes student interests and voices at their center. As the example with Dante at the beginning of this chapter illustrates, the classrooms that many of our students have experienced prior to entering secondary ELA classrooms may reinforce traditional notions of power and suppress opportunities for students to *see* and *hear* themselves reflected within the classroom context. However, a *re-designed* classroom can also offer multiple entry points for participation, spaces for peer collaboration, and layouts that feel equitable and democratic (to hark back to the pose of Chapter 3).

EXCAVATING A SPACE THAT IS MEANINGFUL FOR ALL

While we want to be clear that intentional design of classroom space is *difficult*—at our university most of the desks are bolted in place, forcing students into regimented straight-ahead formation—making a space conducive for learning does not require a bulldozer or an interior design degree. (A can of paint, on the other hand, can go a long way!) Classroom design is more than desks, chairs, and the perilous stacking of these two in the back of a room Jenga-style in hopes that students will liberate their learning through untangling the mess. The following questions emphasize that design is about *considering how classrooms re-create and reinforce and remediate bodies and relationships in classrooms:*

- What is the visual focus of the classroom? Is it the board? Does this visual focus have the most power? Is it students within the classroom?

- Are objects easy to find when they are needed?
- Does this environment reinforce the lived experiences and values of your community of learners in positive or negative ways?
- How does your classroom welcome students of all backgrounds?
- How are diverse learning needs addressed implicitly within the space?
- What are the *intrinsic* cues for learning and critical engagement within the classroom space?

The classroom is the foundation for learning. This may sound unduly theoretical, but we are reminded that we often gloss over the classroom as a space we're given rather than a space we construct. As a result, many teacher education programs begin from a faulty foundation; if we have not used the questions above to examine our own classrooms, we make it harder for the educators and learners in these spaces to do the same.

As a student teacher, Antero sat in a friend's classroom admiring his posters of popular musicians, revolutionaries, and literary greats. This teacher remarked, "Wait until you have your own classroom, you'll see. It's not cheap." Fast-forwarding 6 years, Antero arrived at school early one day to witness his friend, Peter, lugging in not one or two or three but four to-be-assembled bookshelves that he had bought at Ikea. Peter was moving past the storage limitations of his classroom on his own terms. Rather than being stuck with the industrial steel of his classroom, he asked his students to build and custom-paint the shelves that would house the books in the classroom. During lunches and after school for the week, students followed the wordless instructions and constructed the bookshelves. They then painted them as they wished, and strategically created the organizational plans for their classroom library. By the time they were done, the students in Peter's class had collectively built a classroom space that looked as they wished and functioned as they desired. Peter's efforts remind us that attempting to improve the possibilities of classroom design involves more than the physical space; the process of designing can be a community-building exercise. Unlike Antero's effort with students at the beginning of the year, Peter's project revolved around a mutual classroom goal: to improve the classroom library and make it look cool.

These reflections on the costs of classroom design and on who gets to make design choices within the classroom hark back to our discussion of classroom design as a means of exerting power and control over students. Posters, for example, are easy pieces to add to classrooms not simply to cover up blemishes but to enhance the interests of students. Stenciled art of hip-hop artists, posters of urban film adaptations of Shakespeare's works, and glossy images of civil rights leaders are powerful ways to create a common vision of the work and interests within a classroom. Given that purchasing posters out of your own pocket can become costly, encouraging students to create their own work, adorning the walls with slogans, and making one-time investments in picture frames can go a long way toward preserving the images that can sustain the work in a classroom from year to year.

Further, clustering desks and creating circles can help mediate concerns around student input. However, this is only a starting place. In her expansive look at colonial and imperial suppression of indigenous knowledge within social science research, Linda Tuhiwai Smith writes, "Space is often viewed in Western thinking as being static or divorced from time. This view generates ways of making sense of the world as a 'realm of stasis,' well-defined, fixed and without politics" (1999, p. 52).

Space is socially constructed, and the physical environment as well as the discourse that emerges within it are bound by the constraints of classroom participants. If a space is ideologically hostile—perhaps it reifies social norms of White privilege, gender inequality, or able-bodiedness—it suppresses learning possibilities. Such denial of participation may be invisible to participants, including you as the educator. Yet as Kevin Leander (2004) reminds us, "classroom interaction, involving literacy practices such as reading, interpretation, writing, image production, and talk, continually produces social space" (p. 117). As you build your classroom space, consider what social justice goals and critical identities are cultivated in your classroom.

DESIGNING FOR DELIGHT

In the opening of *Harlem on Our Minds: Place, Race, and the Literacies of Urban Youth* (2010), Valerie Kinloch describes the enthusiasm with which her students travel to Harlem:

> That summer, the administrators of the Bridge Program in Charlotte had decided to take our graduating high school seniors to New York City. When the seniors were told the news, there was utter joy. Hearts pounded, smiles widened, and excitement filled the air. They were going to New York City and I was going to be a witness, an observer, and a participant in this first experience for them and for me. We were all overjoyed that the community we had read about in the Black Literature course that I had facilitated the year before was going to welcome us with a warm embrace. (pp. 1–2)

How often do our classrooms produce the same heart-pounding excitement and joy? Beyond elementary grades, when have students smiled in anticipation of entering the classroom spaces? Perhaps the reply "almost never" can be attributed to the rote monotony of visiting the same basic classroom, for all practical purposes, year after year. The force of daily habit can dull the passion of entering sites of learning every day. However, just as importantly, consider that the spaces themselves may feel deadening and covered with layers of figurative dust: the shedded skin of years of assumed practices within classrooms. When have the spaces in which you've taught genuinely surprised you or your students?

In our Teaching Reading course at Colorado State University, we assign our students to spend a predetermined class day wandering the local Fort Collins Museum of Discovery. We give no directions other than to take a picture of yourself somewhere in the museum. (Partly, this requirement helps with accountability so that we know students actually went to the museum, and partly we are interested in *where* in the museum they document themselves.) Students come back to class the following week invigorated by the space: They could try out funny looking instruments like a theremin, they could look silly in the tornado-simulating booth, they could build flying devices, and so forth. Essentially, everything in the space encouraged manipulating, listening, playing. As a class, the students describe the space as one that mixes fun with learning. Inevitably, a student brings up the elephant slumbering in the room: *Why can't our classrooms function in similar ways?* So we pose the question to you: What can be tailored within your room to provoke delight?

TECHNOLOGY MEDIATES SPACE

We should also remember that the notion of space is a fluid one. In the 21st century, the learning space begins long before we even enter our classroom. For better or worse, mobile devices and the flurry of online "spaces" infringe on our lives outside of school. A plethora of 1:1 laptop and digital tablet programs and near-ubiquitous mobile media use means students *could* often be engaged in learning in robust ways. As adults, this is certainly the case for us: From perusing emails over coffee to responding to texts at traffic lights to keeping abreast of global news via Twitter as we walk across campus, we communicate differently because of technology, and it changes how we relate to the physical world around us. Having a vibrating, buzzing, often annoying device anchored to our pockets means that we, like our students, are never far away from what is a potentially powerful and public learning environment.

We have written elsewhere about the ways learning shifts in this digital culture (Garcia, 2012; Garcia & O'Donnell-Allen, 2014), but here we want to encourage you to ponder the possibilities for improving your classroom space by recognizing the ways in which technology can be incorporated to amplify student learning. We suggest this as an intentional space for *design*: How does your classroom reflect the predisposed practices and spaces of learning that occur before students enter your school site? Whereas in the past a set of desktop computers in the corner of a classroom could be seen as a luxury, today it would be seen as a bothersome, anachronistic gesture for students to have to pace to that side of the room, launch a web browser, and solicit information for a project. Today, learning possibilities are "personal, portable, pedestrian" (Ito et al., 2006), thanks to mobile devices.

This is not to say that technology should, by any means, replace the learning afforded by face-to-face interaction or the power of teacher-driven instructional design. In fact, many foolhardy attempts at integrating technology in schools hinder meaningful learning experiences. We are concerned with how technology continues to be seen as a band-aid for fixing long-standing educational quagmires. In 2011, Antero's school spent nearly half a million dollars to place SMART Boards in the majority of the classrooms in the school. Because little attention was devoted to preparing teachers to use these devices, however, many of the boards were quickly smudged with the wrong kind of marker, quietly cast aside in the corners of classrooms, and used primarily as bulkier versions of the LCD displays that teachers were already familiar with. It was a huge expense made in the name of improving academics on campus that had significantly underwhelming results. This cycle of racing to *fix* education with fancy technology has been a century-long effort (Cuban, 1986). In a research project with Thomas Philip (Philip & Garcia, 2013, 2014), Antero outlined several powerful ways technology can be brought into classrooms. Re-creating a framework established in their earlier research, he and Philip suggest that decisions about integrating technology into classrooms should ask questions around the "3Ts" of classroom engagement: Text, Tools, and Talk (Philip & Garcia, 2013, pp. 311–314).

- *Text:* What new texts will be introduced by the technology? How are traditional texts altered or remediated through new technologies? Why are these texts important for what students will learn?
- *Tools:* How does the tool offer ways of collecting, representing, visualizing, analyzing, and communicating information that contributes to improved learning? What is the context of learning that makes this tool imperative to students' lives?
- *Talk:* How do we support classroom talk that leverages the texts, tools, and new forms of communication introduced through the technology to support student learning? Are the ways discourse transpires within classrooms made more robust as a result of this tool? How are forms of communication limited?

These questions, taken collectively, do not offer strict yes/no guidelines about what kinds of learning and technology integration should happen in classrooms. However, the considerations outlined here behoove individual educators as well as districts as a whole to consider the *intent* behind using technology in schools. Within the context of this pose, these three groups of questions can serve as useful tools for reaching flow in the pose of Teacher as Designer. They can help you design contexts for technology use that meaningfully build democratic and humanizing relationships within the classroom. These questions contribute to one holistic classroom design question: What are the ways that technologies in your classroom reframe *how* students read, compose, and meaningfully communicate in contemporary society? Further, what kinds of life, civic, and work experiences is your classroom preparing students for?

SPACE, MORALE, AND MORALITY

Space has an emotional impact on all of us. Where do you feel comfortable? How do you construct an environment that is familiar, welcoming, safe for yourself? Maybe you have pictures on the walls around you? Maybe post-it notes offer encouragement? In Chapter 4 we described the environments in which we write; the ambient hum of coffee shop noise or the cacophony of punk rock help us work comfortably. At the same time, we inherently recognize when spaces do not feel welcoming to us. While the tabula rasa of an unadorned classroom can offer possibilities for humanizing pedagogy, it can also be overwhelming. Even more importantly, as teachers we often feel powerless to control aspects of our classroom. Antero would often unintentionally make his students giggle when—after regularly receiving phone calls that interrupted the class—he would disconnect his phone from the jack in the wall. (Often this would simply mean that his class was interrupted when a student aide knocked on his door to deliver the message that would have arrived via phone call!)

Antero often migrated from classroom to classroom throughout the school day because the teachers outnumbered the classrooms. Building a comfortable environment within the constraints of another teacher's room proved challenging. A converted auto-shop classroom on campus housed two classes simultaneously (see Figure 6.1).

Figure 6.1. A Converted Auto-Shop Classroom Houses Two Classes Simultaneously

Prior to building his Ikea-shelved classroom, Antero's colleague Peter dealt with moving constantly from one class to another by constructing an elaborate wheeled desk that contained all of the materials each of his classes would need. This lumbering behemoth would be pushed from one room to another, slowly, deliberately. Peter named the contraption the Armadillo.

Similarly, when Cindy was teaching at the high school level, she was asked to move from a very nice classroom to the worst area of a very old school building because her section of the school was being remodeled. To add insult to injury, she learned that even when the remodeling was complete, she wouldn't get her original classroom back because that section of the building would now house the Business Department. This meant that for the first quarter of the school year, her new "classroom" would be located in the busiest end of the school library, with the Latin teacher conducting her classes on the opposite end and a Special Ed teacher consulting with students in the middle. Further complicating matters was the fact that the library would be operating as usual during her class time. This meant that librarians would be checking out books and giving book talks sotto voce to entire classes about 30 feet away from Cindy's area. Students would be roaming the shelves looking for books, and the reference section 10 feet away from her classroom space would be in full swing when other classes were looking for sources for their research papers.

Although these circumstances were not ideal, to the say the least, Cindy had no choice but to comply. This made it difficult to enact principles central to her teaching—to create with students an atmosphere that enables them to openly share their thinking about the texts they are reading and writing; to listen attentively and challenge respectfully others' thoughts and questions; and to engage in the process of collaborating and constructing understanding together. The new classroom arrangement not only challenged these principles, but had the potential to make it physically impossible to maintain them.

After some initial venting, Cindy eventually remembered to breathe and recognized that although it was true that she and her students wouldn't be the direct beneficiaries of the remodeling, the building was in drastic need of improvement, something her colleagues and other students at the school would enjoy. She returned to her pose around designing a positive classroom culture and determined that this problem was too big to solve alone, especially because her students would wobble around it daily, too. Besides, designing classroom culture should never be just the teacher's purview, but a joint endeavor with students. She determined that while she had to comply with the demand to move, she could respond mindfully.

While she always began the school year by asking students to contribute to class norms as described in Chapter 2, this time she explained the reasons for the students' dislocation (and they weren't happy either). She asked them to help her identify the pros and cons of their new classroom space and to develop norms in light of these conditions. Students determined that there were actually some advantages. For example, the close proximity of the reference area and library computers made research more accessible, so what if Cindy moved the senior research paper to the first quarter rather than waiting until later in the year? Likewise, because librarians were just a few steps away, why not use them as resources more frequently than students would if they had been in a normal classroom space? Admittedly, the noise level would be a challenge if a single person (e.g., Cindy or a student presenter) was facilitating the class at the front of the room, so what if they moved the furniture, or sat on the floor in a tight circle when necessary? What if they moved to tables for small-group activities and rotated among these tables roundtable-style when individual students were in charge of leading discussions or making presentations?

While these solutions weren't always ideal because the library was as noisy as ever, when Cindy's students moved into a regular classroom during the second quarter, the accommodations they had made when holding their class in the library had lasting and positive effects. Students' impressions of the library had improved because they saw it as a more active, inviting space; likewise they now viewed librarians as resources for their learning rather than people preoccupied with shushing them. Classroom interactions shifted as well, because students expected to take on a more facilitative role than they might have in a conventional classroom space.

Unfortunately, Cindy's classroom conditions worsened even more during the second semester, when her class moved to the far wing of the 40+-year-old school to inhabit a room vacated by the Business Department. When she took her students to visit their new digs toward the end of the first semester as their class was still meeting in the library, they were uncharacteristically silent. And then the anger set in. At least the library had been pleasant with its carpet and comfy chairs, but the new classroom was dismal. Water didn't just leak from the discolored ceiling when it rained, it gushed. The walls were dingy gray and stained from water damage, and many of the floor tiles were crumbling or missing altogether. An enormous pillar stood in the middle of the room, blocking any nearby line of sight. The desks were actually old typewriter tables (yes, typewriters) with removable panels that inevitably pinched one's fingers when they needed to be adjusted. If no one cared about this physical space, students wondered, did they care about their well-being? Did they care about their learning?

In the end, Cindy and her students were determined to exploit the advantages of being relocated to the most isolated area of the school. From all appearances, there was nowhere to go but up. Cindy asked students to imagine the room they would design if money were no object, and they brainstormed accoutrements for a comfortable, decidedly un-school-like space, complete with flexible seating, plush furniture and carpet, natural elements like plants, and brightly colored walls filled with art.

Because money (or more accurately, the lack thereof) was indeed a concern for Cindy and her students, the next step was to figure out how they could create a space with similar design elements on an almost nonexistent budget. So, at the students' suggestion, Cindy passed around a penny jar every day at the beginning of class, wherein students could dump pocket change. After a while, the donations added up. When the student council was gathering items for their annual garage sale, Cindy's students cherry-picked a comfy old sofa and a cool leather chair and end table. She found a knock-off Persian rug at a warehouse sale, and students brought in other donations from home, including an aquarium and a microwave. Cindy contributed two huge houseplants of her own and used some of the students' donations to buy paint and supplies so that students with artistic skills could create a "sky wall" with pale blue paint and sponge-painted clouds. They also transformed the unsightly pillar into a tree trunk covered with vines and continued the vine motif around the chalkboard. As for art, student projects routinely covered the walls.

All of these elements combined to create a unique, comfortable, and surprisingly flexible space that could be reconfigured depending on the task at hand or the mode of interaction most appropriate for student learning. The typewriter desks were arranged in a U-shape around the room, with the couch, leather chair, and rug as a focal point facing the chalkboard, creating a natural space for student presentations. Because chairs weren't attached to the tables, students could easily move them into a circle for whole-group discussions. The typewriter tables could also be pushed together in pods for small-group discussions or to create flat surfaces when students were working on multimodal projects. Cindy's file cabinets and desk (which she never sat at anyway) were pushed into an unobtrusive corner. Microwave popcorn was an almost daily snack, and students often came in during lunch to warm up food and hang out. Despite the fact that the ceiling still leaked and the floor tiles still crumbled, students took ownership of the space. To this day, the room remains Cindy's favorite of any she's ever taught in.

And while it was small contributions from students that added up and helped revitalize Cindy's classroom, you don't have to rely on donations from students or parents to construct a wholesome and collaboratively developed space. Instead, look for furniture that can be salvaged or local businesses that may be looking to make donations to a worthy cause, and never underestimate the potential of a generous lick of paint in significantly transforming the environment. As both Cindy and Antero can attest, getting your hands dirty alongside your students creates a powerful, trusting space and encourages students to feel invested in the classroom where they will be spending a large part of their year.

Taking the dingy conditions of the school into his own hands, a teacher at Antero's school similarly looked for solutions to spatial challenges. One year, an art teacher envisioned walls that offered student artwork and voices, which could be built upon from year to year. Starting with silhouettes of themselves that students traced and painted colorfully, the mural covering the halls of the school slowly grew in complexity over several years (see

Figure 6.2). Some silhouettes had protest signs or balloons added to their hands. Later, abstract shapes and complex stenciled art were added. In a powerful move, the teacher reached out to local muralists and graffiti artists who were invited onto the campus to add to the building-long, multistoried mural (see Figure 6.3). The work was a years-long collaboration of students and noteworthy artists, and it was unlike anything the students had seen before. Yes, occasionally students would tag the work with the graffiti of local gangs, but the teacher would touch up or cover the work as necessary. And, unlike other spaces on campus, the mural garnered much less "tagging" than places that didn't have student voices represented on them.

Figure 6.2. Remixed Student Outlines Holding Protest Signs and Balloons Mingle with Other Artistic Contributions in the Halls of Antero's High School

Figure 6.3. The Work of Local Muralists and Graffiti Artists Mix with Student Contributions

Throughout the year, students could be seen pointing to a faceless figure or a geometric invention with pride, telling a friend that that was their contribution. At least in one building on campus, the voices, interests, and creative contributions of the students at the school could be seen by everyone who entered. This work was not without controversy. As a socially loaded form of speech and expression within South Central Los Angeles (and globally), graffiti art is hotly contested culturally and legally (Phillips, 1999; Sanchez-Tranquilino, 1995). With the turnover of administrative leadership, the murals were painted over during a summer between school years. Sadly, authoritarian adult control was exerted once again over the halls, but the pictures here depict the artifacts of an era when youth voice guided the spaces of the school.

Though we could simply take this assertion of authoritarian control as an example of a failed experiment, we'd rather point to a few key characteristics that made the work successful in hopes that you might incorporate them as you work toward flow within the Teacher as Designer pose:

1. The project was guided by teacher vision: Specifically, this work fit into how one teacher perceived design as cultural advocacy.
2. The work was iterative: A wholly-formed mural did not show up on the walls of the school one day. Such a notion is counter to the collaborative intent of a project that echoed years of student and community participation.
3. The work fostered community voice: Students saw their work as linked to the artists they saw and admired on the streets and in galleries throughout Los Angeles.

Ultimately, co-construction of deliberate design among students, teachers, and community allows for similar co-construction of imperative curricular work within the classroom. The design work here—as with Cindy's efforts moving from one end of the school to another—led to powerful community-building and instructional elements within the classroom. What's the lesson to be learned?

Space is a place to start from and build upon.

When designing classroom environments and learning experiences, the morale the classroom space fosters needs to be considered. Particularly in the current politically fraught climate for the teaching profession, we must make sure our classroom spaces are developed in collaboration with our students. We are reminded that the continuing, ongoing narratives of struggle that we experience in our schools exist in many other contexts: Cindy's ultimately positive experience that came from ongoing frustration with spaces in her schools; Antero's continual upheaval from one classroom to another; an art teacher's powerful, multiyear mural extinguished over a summer with the turnover of administration. In looking at these examples we want to weave together two principal concerns—classroom *morale* and *morality*. With space conditions constantly in flux, the duress of the situation is a cause of concern for all of us. At the same time, the way such upheaval can occur with the change of an administration or with a change in district interests makes us question the morality around such decisions.

Advocating for classroom spaces on behalf of our students and ourselves is about creating a classroom that reflects our system of personal values and political intent *within* a classroom space. Yes, culturally relevant posters, community-focused desk clustering, and works that share student voices help build community. However, these efforts *also* suggest how classrooms must be spaces for teacher advocacy and culturally proactive pedagogy that honor and reflect youth voices.

SPILLING OVER DEMOCRATIC POSSIBILITIES: CULTURE BEYOND THE CLASSROOM

While you may be on your way to making a class*room* that is enticing to all your students, the pose of Teacher as Designer does not stop at the threshold of your teaching space. *Within* this space, what classroom structures and practices do you need to develop or hack to encourage democratic engagement? Harking back to Chapter 2 on hacking, we are aware of the tricky power dynamics that emerge in classrooms and schools. However, in addition to the work teachers must do to amplify and encourage voices within the classroom, our responsibility is also to support students in out-of-classroom spaces as well.

In light of these considerations, we want teachers to ponder how they can use their school resources and their own expertise as potential *sponsors of literacy* (Brandt, 2001). In her formative work around this term, Deborah Brandt describes *sponsors of literacy* as "agents, local or distant, abstract or concrete, who enable, support, teach, model, recruit, regulate, suppress, or withhold literacy and gain advantage by it in some way" (p. xiii). It is important to recognize here that sponsors of literacy are spaces, individuals, and objects. We can intentionally cultivate and sponsor literacy as teachers and as librarians (see Hamilton, 2013). At the same time, our classrooms can function as sponsors of literacy that draw in the interests and voices of both students and outside community members. In revisiting our notion of culturally proactive education, we must consider how our classrooms can be sponsors of literacy that mediate fluid engagement with community literacies *beyond* our classrooms. As such, a discussion of classroom learning and design must consider how such work can build pathways for engagement beyond the walls of the school.

Questioning the out-of-school spaces of literacy in a study on Latino youth, Elizabeth Birr Moje (2004) asks, "What *is* a space? Is it constituted by material conditions? Or is a space what it is because of the people who occupy the space?" (p. 15). Building off of this notion, we are reminded of the civic lessons that can emerge when we open up our classrooms to the world of our local and global community, as discussed in Chapter 3. In this sense, we can connect with Moje's observation that "all spaces are in some sense 'literate' spaces" (p. 16). Harking back to an earlier point in this chapter, technology *tools* can deliberately design portals of participation among your classroom, the community, and far-off experts. Video conferencing with local and national political leaders, tweeting to popular authors, and blogging all open up spaces for youth interests that make the literacies *within* ELA classrooms extend deliberately beyond typical classrooms. Using 21st-century tools to demolish these 20th-century borders is just as much a part of your role as a designer as building new spaces.

At the same time, we must be aware of how our classrooms can work around limitations of technology as well. A few summers ago, we worked with 4th-grade students as part of the "Saving Our Stories (SOS) Project." Sponsored by the Colorado State University Writing Project, the SOS Project is oriented toward engaging students in "saving" the stories of the local Fort Collins Latino community that might otherwise go untold. As the lead teachers in the program, we invited the students, most of them bilingual Spanish speakers, to become "secret agents" with the mission of uncovering these stories to share with others beyond our classroom. For three weeks, students considered the following questions:

- What does our city look like today?
- What did it look like in the past?
- What might it look like in the future? And who gets to decide?

We were initially enthused about teaching the class in a school computer lab. However, within minutes of instruction, we realized that the bulky tables that the desktop computers perched on functioned more as a design challenge than as the opportunity we initially perceived. Conceptualizing the classroom as a "makerspace" (see Chapter 2), however, prompted us to designate the open area near the front of the room as a collaborative workspace. This decision ultimately liberated the expectations of the class to be jointly designed. By the end of the first week of class, this space was a cluttered, yet functional, mess of cardboard boxes salvaged from local dumpsters, scissors, duct tape, and student-created blueprints for a cardboard city that reflected the past, present, and future of Fort Collins (see Figure 6.4).

In addition to building the cardboard city, students enacted a "maker mindset" (Dougherty, n.d.) throughout the SOS Project by developing and exploring stories through myriad forms, including print-based texts, such as daily journals and odes modeled on the work of Pablo Neruda and Gary Soto; digital texts like podcasts, movies, and slide shows; and a host of multimodal texts, including an equity quilt (made of foam squares), board games, and "sidewalk chalk tweets" that we posted to Twitter. The cardboard city, however, was the text students added to throughout the workshop as their

Figure 6.4. Elementary Students Construct a Cardboard City Remixing the Past, Present, and Future of Fort Collins, CO

understanding of Fort Collins—and their place within it—evolved. As such, it offers an example of classroom space being used to complicate student understanding of their local community.

After begging cardboard donations from local big-box stores (and engaging in a fair amount of shameless dumpster-diving for cardboard on our own), we initiated construction of the cardboard city during the first week of the workshop, as students were thinking and writing about stories in their own present lives as well as those of their families. We asked them to consider places that were important to them that they felt ought to be included in the city. Armed with duct tape and plastic screws, hinges, and saws from Makedo kits, students got to work. They collaborated in small groups to determine a building they wanted to construct and to draw up plans. Soon the classroom was transformed into a loud, busy workshop as students shouted out directions to one another, negotiated over pieces of cardboard, and sawed and assembled their creations.

As their buildings took shape, we began to gain glimpses of Fort Collins from a kids'-eye view. Among the buildings they deemed important were an apartment building where one student lived, their school, a church, and a local Burger King (complete with a drive-through window). For the next phase of their construction, students focused on the history of Fort Collins and constructed buildings representing the city's past.

To provide historical context for this work, we also visited spaces outside of the classroom, taking students on field trips to two local museums. The first was El Museo de las Tres Colonias, a small restored adobe home in the northern part of the city that was occupied in the early part of the 20th century by migrant workers employed at the Great Western Sugar Beet factory. During their visit, students used iPads to capture digital pictures and video of the museum and its numerous artifacts and pictures of local Latino families through the years. In addition to touring the tiny three-room home, students also heard the stories of Chuck Solano, who worked in the sugar beet fields as a child. Chuck pointed out that the room in the house with the hard dirt floor functioned as the pantry and "refrigerator" since it was cooler and the family had no access to conventional refrigeration. He also shared the less frequently told stories of Fort Collins's racially fraught past when signs like "No Mexicans, No Dogs" were hung in local businesses on the city's main street. Surprised by both the tour and Chuck's stories, students began developing a better sense of the importance of saving and sharing these stories with others.

The following week, students gained a very different perspective on these stories when they toured the Fort Collins Museum of Discovery, a combined history and science museum. They received a private tour of the museum archives, where they viewed historic maps and photographs of the city, as well as personal photos of Latino citizens dating from the 1930s. They also discovered that the history of local migrant farmers was represented in the form of a life-sized model of a sugar beet shack that even housed a videotaped interview with Chuck Solano. The exhibit's location in the back corner of the museum, however, made it less inviting than the other, more interactive areas on the museum floor, and ambient noise bouncing off the high ceilings of the building made it impossible to hear the interview.

Deliberate inquiry into the contrasts between the design decisions made in the tiny El Museo space and those made in the well-funded Museum of Discovery allowed students to consider whose stories get foregrounded in public spaces and whose stories are obscured in the city's past. In this sense, physical environments—the historic streets and current structures of Fort Collins *and* the cardboard-cluttered classroom now disentangled from the computer workstations—became connected to ELA and civic concepts of story, identity, and advocacy.

Collecting notes and thoughts from their field trip research, the class began construction of cardboard buildings to represent Fort Collins's past. Some students simply built representations of historic structures that were still standing, like the Great Northern Hotel in Old Town and a working trolley, suspended from a duct tape cable. Another group felt it was important to include El Museo. Yet another group built city hall, but with one important addition: At the suggestion of a video documentarian who had joined us that week, students cut out a large hole on one side of the box. This side functioned as a movie theater of sorts when they inserted an iPad that played videos and slide shows the students had recorded previously in the workshop. In the final week of the workshop, students built structures they envisioned as part of the city's future. These more whimsical structures included Lego contraptions and a homework machine. At the party on the final day of the workshop, students assembled the entire city with their buildings and contraptions from past, present, and future Fort Collins.

As one component of the SOS Project, the cardboard city demonstrates that even very young children are capable of developing age-appropriate skills for re-appropriating history, critiquing inequities, and imagining alternative views based on whose stories matter and how these stories figure (or do not figure) into a city's design. Space and designing space became a kind of text for students to read, interpret, produce, and remix. The principal dispositions of many of the poses across this book comingled with intentional efforts to de-center the traditionally designed school computer lab by transforming it into a makerspace. Though much of the "work" of the SOS Project was produced within the classroom makerspace, this work relied upon synthesis of students' lived experiences within their Fort Collins community, their encounters with local archives and museums, the research they conducted, and their own expectations about what the world *can* be when they put into action a proactive, equitable vision that mixes past, present, and future within the same space.

CONCLUSION: SPACE IS NOT THE FINAL FRONTIER

Returning to Elizabeth Moje's 2004 study, we are reminded that "space matters, not just for the physical environment it provides . . . , but also in terms of the meanings, relationships, and identities to be made in these spaces" (p. 31). As we offer examples of times when we wobbled within our own school about the seeming fixity of classroom spaces—uprooted from familiar environments, finding it difficult to maneuver or build community—we wonder how newer teachers are guided toward intentional design and agency around the spaces they work within. What's more, if teachers feel powerless to design classroom spaces and learning experiences, we can only imagine how the students feel. As you continue to wobble within the pose of Teacher as Designer, don't hesitate to draw from and adapt the inventive strategies, borne mostly of necessity, that the teachers in this chapter used to establish flow. Most importantly, remember that being deliberate about the design of your classroom space involves more than rearranging the chairs: It offers a powerful opportunity to shape your teaching and your students' learning.

PROVOCATIONS

1. Take inventory of your classroom space, furniture, and resources. How does your environment provoke curiosity and student interest? How does it reflect the lives of your classroom community? What could you change about this space to better engage in culturally proactive learning?

2. Moving beyond your own classroom, create an asset map of your school and nearby community spaces. What are the areas in and around this environment that can support powerful learning processes? How can these be utilized within your classroom?

3. As you build your classroom space, what social justice goals and critical identities are cultivated in your classroom? How do you build a classroom culture where vulnerable learning mentioned in Chapter 2 can take place?

4. What are the narratives about schooling that are learned through traversing your school's campus? How does it feel walking from the parking lot to the office to your classroom? What about for students? What spaces are students found most frequently congregating around? What spaces feel neglected? What would it take to transform these spaces?

5. More metaphorically, what do you perceive to be the space you inhabit within the teaching profession? Do you see this as a space that other teachers look to for support or guidance? Do you find any spaces in your profession stifling, limiting? What could you (and allies) do to expand this space?

Connections

Explore the following resources for further insight into spatial design:

Shor, Ira. (1987). *Critical Teaching and Everyday Life.*

>Primarily a theoretical look at critical pedagogy within U.S. contexts, Shor's book offers several salient examples and protocols for teachers to use within classrooms to deconstruct power dynamics.

Lego, Minecraft, graph paper

>Regardless of your own skills and technical know-how, nothing beats building, sketching, and exploring the spatial possibilities of what your classroom can be. Start by sketching out the physical constraints of your room: the walls, doors, and windows. Now start moving pieces of furniture and desks in your model. Consider how each new configuration changes the dynamics of learning.

The Quiet Year (buriedwithoutceremony.com/the-quiet-year/)

>A game of culture-building and map construction played with a deck of cards and a single sheet of paper, *The Quiet Year* invites players to sketch out the year of a civilization on a map. The collaborative process yields surprising insight into how players see societies interacting and interpret their relationship to nearby resources.

The Elusive Decisive Moment

One of Antero's good friends, Dorka, is a professional photographer. When visiting her, it isn't uncommon for her face to be obscured by a large camera with an equally large telephoto lens. She documents everything masterfully, always attempting to capture that "decisive moment" (Cartier-Bresson, 1952) that represents the *essence* of a human subject. It is an elusive and fleeting moment, and Dorka is adept at tapping her finger on the camera's trigger at *just* the right time. In addition to being a photographer, Dorka is an incredible mother, and her son, Linus (four at the time we write this), often trails behind her clinging to her leg, avoiding eye contact with strangers if possible. His attention to strangers can, too, be elusive and fleeting. Watching his mother, Linus can mimic the ways she takes a photo. Placing his hands near his face, making clockwise motions, he will adjust the lens, and finally—when the moment is just right—his index finger taps the invisible trigger. He might make the audible click himself, signaling an imaginary masterpiece filed away for free developing.

But Linus—inasmuch as he is a documentarian of the world with his imaginary camera—is something of an anomaly. His use of his invisible camera differs significantly from the way many of his peers—those youth born circa the second decade of the 21st century—will operate theirs. Dorka's work requires her to use a large single-lens camera—a *real* camera. For the overwhelming majority of young adults, a phone is a camera, and also a handheld entertainment system, and a device for sending email. These "cameras," used mostly for snapshots and selfies, bear little resemblance to Linus's imaginary camera. We do not hold them close to the eye and press a shutter button to activate an aperture that will admit only a specific amount of light to shine on a strip of film.

Instead, to take photos like most people do today, you hold the device a foot or so away from your body to optimally frame your subject and then press a button on a touch screen. The screen may blink (or even mimic the sound of a single-lens camera) to indicate the photo has been taken. It may not. Consequently, when most children pretend to take a photo today, they reproduce this action and will continue to do so until the next gadget dictates a new process. As our devices are fundamentally altered, so too are the physical movements we employ to use them.

The same is true for the physical act of reading. In 2011, a YouTube video that went viral showed an infant trying to swipe and interact with a print magazine (UserExperienceWorks). Clearly, the digital tablet had been so omnipresent in this child's life that the norm for media interaction dictated swiping a screen rather than flipping the pages of a paper magazine. As the former sentence indicates, even the vocabulary is different: We "swipe" with our finger to unlock screens or change the image of a digital book. We no longer just swipe credit cards through digital devices (itself a change in vocabulary) or accuse petty thieves of swiping candy from a convenience store. Rather, "swiping" is now an innate part of one's literacy practices. As the physical actions we use to interact with texts change, so too does the vocabulary of reading, learning, and *engaging with* change.

We share the above anecdote to highlight the fact that models of learning and engagement change over time. In addition to highlighting the *physicality* of literacies, changes in these models should also heighten our awareness of the ways that contexts shift. Our revised actions for taking pictures didn't swoop into cultural consciousness and take hold overnight. Rather, it was a gradual manifestation of the new social practices that emerge along with innovations all the time.

Similarly, our teaching practices must keep up with the learning needs and literacy practices of our students as they develop different dexterities and tools to generate and interact with different kinds of texts. As the example of Linus reminds us, if even this one tiny aspect of the mode of media production is different today, a wide universe of multimodal possibilities continually opens up in our classrooms. While this realization can be overwhelming, we must remember to breathe, take inventory of the changing demands required in our role as educators, and prepare to assume new poses or acquire new ones as needs and challenges arise. Anticipate wobble. Momentarily achieve flow. Repeat.

The P/W/F model reflects the nimbleness required of today's educators. It establishes the expectation of change as an inevitable facet of existence in a world that is ever in flux. We can either bemoan this reality and cling to tradition or recognize it as a dynamic opportunity for continual professional growth. Whether aiming for the constantly moving target of culturally proactive teaching or curating an optimal set of texts for an inquisitive or querulous student, our actions in classrooms must constantly evolve. As we noted early on in this book, there is no magic collection of "best practices" out there waiting to be discovered. Instead, there is the much broader sense of a "practice" of your teaching that you must continually deepen, much as a practitioner of yoga does over the span of a lifetime. Within this context, the "best" method you select in any given instructional moment is the one that aligns with the poses you have intentionally taken up in your teaching. Adapting that method according to the learning needs of your individual students will entail wobble. Persisting through and reflecting on that wobble, however, will allow you to experience moments of flow that will in turn sharpen your expertise and capacity for responding to future change.

POSE, WOBBLE, FLOW AS POLITICS

We have emphasized throughout this book that the poses you take—and how you choose to wobble with them—are inescapably political in nature. Each pose is a conscious choice we use to frame the daily work in our classrooms, each wobble a possible revolution. Inciting civic engagement in your classroom and curating controversial texts may be obvious examples of political choice. However, the language you utilize, the ways you design the physical space and community culture in your classroom, and even the clothes you wear are all choices that reflect the myriad political identities in which you are entrenched.

In and of itself, Pose, Wobble, Flow isn't inherently revolutionary. However, we believe it is a model that must be used for revolution and resistance in schools today. The poses we have recommended throughout this book are those intended to speak back to the inequities reproduced in schools and society. From shifting the *purposes* for reading and writing in the classroom toward civic outcomes, to intentionally offering texts that reflect the lived experiences of your students, these poses allow you to take political stances based on your constantly developing pedagogy. These poses are intended to revitalize and transform the world of public education; our individual incremental growth as culturally proactive educators will in aggregate lead toward profession-wide shifts, but only if we demand this change in ourselves and from our peers and colleagues. There is an urgency to this work that demands that we do more than sit back and wait for educational reform to occur much as Beckett's Vladimir and Estragon waited for the elusive Godot.

We've provided guidelines and a framework (in Appendixes A and C) that we hope you will utilize for crafting poses unique to your own classroom practice, and we offer them up with full understanding of the tenuous state of the teaching profession today. Even in the months that we have been writing this book, the world of education and the policies that dictate its practices have changed. Policymakers from both sides of the political aisle employ windy rhetoric to advance partisan priorities regarding high-stakes testing, college and career readiness, and teacher tenure. Yet we and our students—those most directly affected by the repercussions of these decisions—are the ones left out of the endless debates.

In light of constantly changing policies and mandates, we must advocate for our students and teach them to join us in advocating for humane and actualizing conditions for learning in our classrooms and in our world.

Rather than simply complying with standards and adopting a status quo mindset, you can anticipate and enact the poses most needed by the students as you, the lead learner in the room, define them.

In *A Pedagogy for Liberation,* Ira Shor and Paulo Freire (1987) write:

> Education is politics! When a teacher discovers that he or she is a politician, too, the teacher has to ask, "What kind of politics am I doing in the classroom?" That is, in whom am I in favor of being as a teacher? . . . The teacher works in favor of something and against something. Because of that she or he will have another great question, How to be consistent in my teaching practice with my political choice? I cannot proclaim my liberating dream and in the next day be authoritarian in my relationships with the students. (p. 46)

In this context, we ask you: what are the *liberating dreams* that compel the poses you take in your classroom? A passion for literature, for the craft of writing, for the act of teaching is nice. *But passion is not enough.* Even when a pose goes unspoken (and we encourage you instead to name it and claim it), it carefully delineates commitment to the betterment of one's pedagogy in order to address the needs, the wants, and the dreams of our students. In this sense, our selection of poses and the teaching that issues from them cannot be haphazard or changed upon a whim. Both must be oriented toward praxis—critical reflection that results in transformative change.

We cannot overemphasize this point. By various measures, we are in a cultural, social crisis today. Racial persecution, the stratification and thinning of the middle class, and salient examples of violence—symbolic and physical—toward nonheterosexual or transgender members of society run rampant today.

This is not hyperbole:

- On August 9, 2014, Michael Brown, an unarmed teenage black man, was fatally shot multiple times by a police officer. He was one of many unarmed individuals of color killed by the police in 2014 (Townes & Petrohilos, 2014). Other high-profile incidents, such as the death of Eric Garner, a New York resident choked to death by police in July 2014 (shown in a video that was shared virally), made issues of police injustice the subject of ongoing national debate and public demonstrations. Hashtags like #Ferguson, #ICantBreathe, #Baltimore, and #BlackLivesMatter fueled vitriol in both online and physical-world contexts.
- On October 14, 2014, Anita Sarkeesian, an outspoken critic of the sexist portrayals of women in video games, was forced to cancel her announced speaking engagement at Utah State University

after she received death threats. As one of many similar instances Sarkeesian experienced throughout the year, this incident highlights the fervent opposition to female, feminist, and non-heteronormative perspectives within video game writing that exists in our culture. Covered widely as a push by individuals who "see ethical problems among game journalists and political correctness in their coverage," the resistance to critics like Sarkeesian continues under the hashtag #GamerGate (Wingfield, 2014).

- On December 28, 2014, 17-year-old transgender teen Leelah Alcorn committed suicide (Johnston, 2014). A note published on her Tumblr page assures readers, "Please don't be sad, it's for the better. The life I would've lived isn't worth living in . . . because I'm transgender." Alcorn concludes her letter with very direct instructions: "My death needs to mean something. My death needs to be counted in the number of transgender people who commit suicide this year. . . . Fix society. Please."

Occurring in only a 6-month period in a single year in the second decade of the 21st century, these incidents combine to form a snapshot for youth that reflects how identity is bound up in cultural instability in today's world. But the snapshot is only unique with regard to the specific vagaries and depictions of dehumanization we bore witness to in that particular year. As you read this, there are surely other examples of oppressive social actions that are plaguing marginalized communities locally and globally. It is clear that our working-class families, youth of color, and individuals who resist heteronormative identities are particularly endangered. Their vulnerability extends beyond whether or not they will matriculate into the realms of higher education where they will be prepared to travel down 21st-century pathways on their way to a coveted, high-paying career. It applies to their chances of safely *existing* as members of U.S. society.

It is in light of the very real consequences of misogyny, patriarchy, sexism, racism, and other oppressions our youth experience today that we consider posing, wobbling, and flowing to be such necessary elements of our teaching practice. Identifying the realities of our students' lives confirms the need to alter and refine that practice on an ongoing basis. Even in the uber-competitive landscape of globalized capitalism, we must sustain vibrant ecosystems and spaces for our students' learning. We must equip ourselves with the necessary tools that will enable us to furnish our students with the tools *they* need so that we can all critique injustice and take social action to transform the world. This is why we must pose, wobble, and flow. As Allan Johnson (2001) explains, "There is no such thing as doing nothing. There is no such thing as being neutral or uninvolved. At every moment, social life involves each of us" (p. 132).

STRIVING FOR THE UNATTAINABLE

Neither of us—Cindy nor Antero—has had a perfect year of teaching. Ever. No matter how close we got to near-continuous moments of flow, there were always moments in which we were let down by ourselves, by our students, and by the often unattainable expectations imposed on failing schools. Students would break our hearts. *Life* outside of school would interfere at the least opportune of times. Our bodies and our minds would fail us in the exhaustion of teaching, most often in that final mad dash to the end of the year. Yet we stubbornly maintain that the year we think we've figured it all out is the year we need to get out of education, since this is a profession that demands perpetual change and professional growth. Every year we must enter the classroom renewed with an absolute faith that the students we face can and will change the world. We must aspire toward the promise of perfect engagement, even if we never achieve it. And we must learn from the ways that our teaching practice deviates from the impossibly perfect throughout the year.

As we noted in our discussion of Dewey's work in Chapter 3, the world of schools remains stubbornly ineffective at "catching up" with the rest of the world outside the schoolhouse walls. Although we have written this book to suggest new ways of approaching the practice of teaching in today's classrooms, we can imagine these poses as a means for reorienting the larger structures of schooling as well. Imagine how schools *could* be transformed if administrators, teachers, and parents worked in parallel around ensuring that a school spent its years wobbling with cultural proactivity. Or with creating a civically engaged citizenry. This approach would involve more than achieving "student learning outcomes" or proving "annual yearly progress" in the narrow terms misguided educational policies currently define. It would require developing schoolwide processes to allow all stakeholders to set personal egos aside, engage in often-difficult conversations, and develop workable action plans that reflect the complex needs of a school.

While we would like to push for these schoolwide visions of P/W/F (and we do so on a regular basis through the professional development we facilitate in schools), we also think that individual poses are inherently personal. We all struggle *differently*. How Antero wobbles with culturally proactive engagement in his courses at Colorado State University varies significantly from how Cindy does. We are equipped with the same tools of engagement, and both seek to remain apprised of the latest literacy and education research. And yet the nuances of our wobbles fluctuate. Like Linus mimicking an archaic form of photography and like the toddler swiping for new content on old media, our practices are constantly *catching up* to where our students are. We sometimes are able to draft behind our students' momentum, and to enjoy momentary flow as a result.

Like Linus learning to adjust his imaginary camera equipment, we are enmeshed in literacy practices that seem innovative now, but may be arcane in the future. As an example, regardless of your age, it's likely that the physical technologies you use as a writer have changed in your lifetime. Maybe you, too, learned to write using a fat No. 2 pencil and dashed paper, and even though you got a grade for penmanship on your report card, your evenly printed lines, then your cursive loops and swirls eventually evolved into a less sophisticated scrawl. Were you required to take "Typing" in high school? Are you of the "word processor" generation, or did your foray into digital writing in school begin on a computer, a desktop, a laptop, or a tablet (or whatever the tool du jour is as you're reading this book now)? If you are like many others in today's society, your informal writing has become a thumb-driven activity. You tap out text messages at stoplights with a single hand (hoping you won't be ticketed if such activities are illegal where you live). Produce, publish, and communicate in an effective vernacular in the time it takes opposing traffic to swim upstream.

BRB. K. Thx.

In light of today's demands related to ever-changing literacies, we elaborated on only six poses:

- Culturally Proactive Teaching
- Teacher as Hacker
- Literacy as Civic Action
- Teacher as Writer
- Teacher as Curator
- Teacher as Designer

Yet each of these poses could (and should) merit a lifetime of exploration. Remember, a pose is not a stagnant state. You don't receive your "Teacher as Writer" merit badge after successfully surviving your first National Novel Writing Month. There is no trophy (that we know of) for being the most adept teacher as hacker. Thus, as your competence in a given pose grows, we hope that you will challenge yourself to keep refining it, and that you will add new poses to your practice as the demands of education and the needs of your students require.

While you'll wobble in either case, we can imagine the lasting utility of using the Pose, Wobble, Flow model to point a spotlight on areas of growth and struggle in your daily classroom practice and to help you achieve staying power and continuous engagement over a lifetime of teaching.

Don't forget: You gotta wobble if you ever want to flow.

Pose, Wobble, Flow Template and Assignment

The Pose, Wobble, Flow assignment is one that we both have used in our teacher education program at Colorado State University, though the following version was adapted by Antero specifically for his Teaching Composition course. It offers a template for designing your own poses and noting your growth with them.

THE POSE, WOBBLE, FLOW ASSIGNMENT

This week you have read a description of teacher development called Pose, Wobble, Flow. The model is one that I feel can help lend vocabulary to the continually changing nature of the profession you are entering. And, while we didn't discuss this early on, you have been attempting various poses—as both writers and educators—throughout this semester. For example, one pose you have taken on (and likely wobbled with for the past 15 weeks) is a pose called "Teacher as Writer." In general, this pose requires you to attempt to write regularly in the same ways you will expect your students to do when you enter the classroom. The word counts imposed on your blogging, as frustrating as they may seem, have been a deliberate prompt for you to wobble with one form of professional development. Under my guidance throughout the semester, you have taken on other poses (and hopefully felt moments of flow with them as well): You looked at writing instruction as a civic activity, as an opportunity for enacting multimodal pedagogy, and as an occasion for peer-supported lesson development.

In the foundations of critical pedagogy, as outlined by Paulo Freire, the act of naming and labeling and *inscribing* the world around you is a necessary and political act. The Pose, Wobble, Flow assignment, coming at the end of an arduous semester for many of you, is one that allows you to name and support the various poses you will undertake in the next phase of your teaching career.

In this assignment you will identify 5 poses: 2 poses you have undertaken over the past semester (perhaps from those listed above) and 3 poses you will carry forward with you as a teacher of writing.

Pose 1 (that you undertook over the past semester):

_____

Pose 2 (that you undertook over the past semester):

_____

Pose 3 (that you will attempt and wobble with in the future):

_____

Pose 4 (that you will attempt and wobble with in the future):

_____

Pose 5 (that you will attempt and wobble with in the future):

_____

For poses 1 and 2 above, you will:

- Name the pose at the top of a sheet of paper;
- Identify 3–5 key principles of this pose;
- Reflect on how you wobbled with this pose over the course of the semester;
- Identify moments of flow;
- Conclude with how this pose will affect your pedagogy moving forward as an educator.

In order to complete these tasks, I would imagine that you will need to write about 2 pages for each pose.

For poses 3–5, I want you to create a 1-page worksheet for yourself, like the example I've provided below for the pose of Teacher as Writer. You will:

- Name the new pose at the top of a sheet of paper;
- Identify 3–5 key principles of this pose;
- Write a one-paragraph rationale about why this is a necessary pose for you as a new teacher given the contexts of learning you will be entering (for most of you this means your student teaching placement);
- Write down 2–3 reflective questions for you to revisit throughout the next semester when you are teaching to allow you to evaluate _where_ you are in your stance with this given pose;

- Describe some specific methods you plan to use in order to achieve some measure of flow in regard to this pose—that is to keep growing as a writing teacher.

TEACHER AS WRITER:
DEVELOP AN IDENTITY AS A WRITER WHO TEACHES AND A TEACHER WHO WRITES BY:

➤ engaging regularly in the practice of writing in order to better understand the rewards and challenges your students will experience as writers;

➤ recognizing that assuming a writer identity is essential to educational equity; and

➤ joining a community of writers and committing yourself to sustained professional learning in the area of writing instruction.

Rationale:

Reflective Questions

1. _____

2. _____

3. _____

Strategies for achieving flow:

_____

_____

_____

_____

Summary of Poses

CULTURALLY PROACTIVE TEACHING:
DEVELOP AN IDENTITY AS A CULTURALLY PROACTIVE TEACHER BY:

➤ framing your teaching around a commitment to praxis and questioning existing inequities in schooling and society;

➤ anticipating students' needs within your classroom and adjusting your practice to their interests, developing identities, and cultural expertise;

➤ articulating your own cultural positionality and reflecting on the ways it shapes your teaching and your students' learning;

➤ using the cultural and linguistic backgrounds of your students as resources for their learning; and

➤ teaching critical literacy skills that will help your students understand, critique, and contest systemic inequities and take social action to change them.

TEACHER AS HACKER:
CREATE AND SUSTAIN A DIALOGIC CURRICULUM
THAT MEETS STUDENTS' LEARNING NEEDS BY:

➤ cultivating a classroom environment that enables vulnerable learning;

➤ emphasizing a production-oriented view of learning that positions students as "makers" and

➤ critically reading one's teaching context and pushing back against systemic constraints that might limit students' learning.

LITERACY FOR CIVIC ENGAGEMENT:
SUPPORT THE DEVELOPMENT OF CIVIC IDENTITY THROUGH LITERACY INSTRUCTION BY:

➤ grounding standards-aligned curricula within current contexts that invite student perspectives and voice;

➤ acknowledging and working through local, national, and historical contexts of power and identity in the texts and writing activities that are encountered within the classroom;

➤ identifying and acting upon the varied positionalities within the classroom—including yours as the educator; and

➤ tying back the components of ELA instruction to the needs of students with regard to power, social capital, and identity within their own public sphere.

TEACHER AS WRITER:
DEVELOP AN IDENTITY AS A WRITER WHO TEACHES AND A TEACHER WHO WRITES BY:

➤ engaging regularly in the practice of writing in order to better understand the rewards and challenges your students will experience as writers;

➤ recognizing that assuming a writer identity is essential to educational equity; and

➤ joining a community of writers and committing yourself to sustained professional learning in the area of writing instruction.

TEACHER AS CURATOR:
INCREASE POWERFUL, CULTURALLY PROACTIVE READING CHOICES WITHIN THE CLASSROOM BY:

➤ disrupting traditional, essentializing, or culturally inaccessible curriculum (sometimes by pushing against the canon);

➤ fostering student choice in reading;

➤ helping students persist through challenges inherent in the act of reading; and

➤ cultivating your own passion for reading.

TEACHER AS DESIGNER:
CREATE MORE EQUITABLE LEARNING ENVIRONMENTS BY DESIGNING AND CODESIGNING THE PHYSICAL AND CULTURAL SPACES OF OUR PRACTICE THROUGH:

➤ sustaining a classroom space—both physical and virtual—that reflects the needs, lives, and interests of your learning community;

➤ building a classroom culture that is safe, welcoming, and democratic;

➤ improvising subversively when schooling conditions shunt you and your students to spaces that would limit learning and diminish morale; and

➤ coconstructing spaces with students for civic learning by drawing on community experts and local resources.

Pose, Wobble, Flow Template

In addition to taking on the poses outlined in this book, this template will allow you to identify your own poses and set guidelines for areas of your practice that you want to intentionally address and wobble with. While the template will certainly work as a tool for your individual reflection, we also encourage you to work through it collaboratively with your own trusted professional learning community. Though each of you may take on different poses (or vary the nuances of similar poses), working on this with a group will allow you to hold one another accountable, share strategies for negotiating wobble, and celebrate moments of flow throughout the school year.

Name your pose here: _____

_____

**(Below, list the 3–5 key principles
that are most important to this pose for you.)**

- _____

- _____

- _____

- _____

- _____

On the next page, you will reflect on the importance of this pose to your development as a teacher and will record possible strategies for wobbling with it over the course of the school year.

Below, write a succinct explanation about why this is a necessary pose for you right now in your teaching. How will this pose help you grow as a teacher? What about this pose gives you *hope* for the powerful work in your classroom?

_____

_____

_____

_____

Write down 2–3 reflective questions that you can revisit throughout the school year that will allow you to evaluate *where* you are in your stance with this given pose:

1. _____

2. _____

3. _____

Finally, describe some strategies you could try when you experience wobble that may lead toward some measure of flow in relation to this pose:

_____

_____

_____

_____

Keep this template in a visible place so that you can revisit it frequently, maintain your commitment toward your pose, and gauge your professional growth.

A free 8½ x 11 version of Appendix C is available
as a PDF file for download and printing at tcpress.com

References

Adichie, C. N. (2009). The danger of a single story. Available at www.ted.com/talks/chimamanda_adichie_the_danger_of_a_single_story/transcript?language=en#t-1064000

Allington, R. L. (2007). Effective teachers, effective instruction. In K. Beers, R. E. Probst, & L. Rief (Eds.), *Adolescent literacy: Turning promise into practice* (pp. 273–288). Portsmouth, NH: Heinemann.

Alvarez, J. (1995). *In the time of the butterflies*. New York, NY: Plume.

Anderson, L. W. (Ed.), Krathwohl, D. R. (Ed.), Airasian, P. W., Cruikshank, K. A., Mayer, R. E., Pintrich, P. R., Raths, J., & Wittrock, M. C. (2001). *A taxonomy for learning, teaching, and assessing: A revision of Bloom's Taxonomy of Educational Objectives*. New York, NY: Longman.

Anstey, M., & Bull, G. (2006). *Teaching and learning multiliteracies: Changing times, changing literacies*. Newark, DE: International Reading Association.

Anyon, J. (2009). Critical pedagogy is not enough: Social justice education, political participation, and the politicization of students. In M. W. Apple, W. Au, & L. A. Gandin (Eds.), *The Routledge international handbook of critical education* (pp. 389–395). New York, NY: Routledge.

Applebee, A. N. (1992). Stability and change in the high-school canon. *English Journal, 81*(5), 27–32.

Applebee, A. N., & Langer, J. A. (2013). *Writing instruction that works: Proven methods for middle and high school classrooms*. New York, NY: Teachers College Press.

Atwell, N. (2014). *In the middle: A lifetime of learning about writing, reading, and adolescents* (3rd ed.). Portsmouth, NH: Heinemann.

Ayers, W., & Alexander-Tanner, R. (2010). *To teach: The journey, in comics*. New York, NY: Teachers College Press.

Bakhtin, M. M. (1986). *Speech genres and other late essays* (Vern W. McGee, trans.). Austin, TX: University of Texas Press.

Barthelme, D. (1997). "Not knowing." In K. Herzinger (Ed.), *Not knowing: The essays and interviews of Donald Barthelme* (pp. 11–24). New York, NY: Random House.

Barton, D., & Hamilton, M. (2000). Literacy practices. In D. Barton, M. Hamilton, & R. Ivanic (Eds.), *Situated literacies: Theorising reading and writing in context* (pp. 16–34). New York, NY: Routledge.

Basbanes, N. (2012). *A gentle madness: Bibliophiles, bibliomanes, and the eternal passion for books*. Chapel Hill, NC: Fine Books Press.

Bell, L. A. (2010). *Storytelling for social justice: Connecting narrative and arts in anti-racist teaching*. New York, NY: Routledge.

Berliner, D. C., & Biddle, B. J. (1995). *The manufactured crisis: Myths, fraud, and the attack on America's public schools.* New York, NY: Perseus Books.

boyd, d. (2014). *It's complicated: The social lives of networked teens.* New Haven, CT: Yale University Press.

Bloom, B. S., Engelhart, M. D., Furst, E. J., Hill, W. H., & Krathwohl, D. R. (Eds.). (1956). *Taxonomy of educational objectives—The classification of educational goals: Handbook 1: cognitive domain.* London, WI: Longmans, Green & Co. Ltd.

Bradbury, R. (2001). 6th annual writer's symposium by the sea. University of California Television. Available at youtube.com/watch?v=_W-r7ABrMYU

Brandt, D. (2001). *Literacy in American lives.* Cambridge, England: Cambridge University Press.

Brick, M. (2012). *Saving the school: The true story of a principal, a teacher, a coach, a bunch of kids, and a year in the crosshairs of education reform.* New York, NY: Penguin Press.

Briggs, X. (2005). *The geography of opportunity: Race and housing choice in metropolitan America.* Washington, DC: Brookings Institution Press.

Burgin, T. (2012). *Yoga for beginners: A quick-start guide to practicing yoga for new students.* [Kindle version]. Available at amazon.com

California Department of Education. (1998). English-language arts content standards for California public schools. Available at cde.ca.gov/be/st/ss/documents/elacontentstnds.pdf

Camangian, P. (2010). Starting with self: Teaching autoethnography to foster critically caring literacies. *Research in the Teaching of English, 45*(2), 179–204.

Carmen, S. (2002). A brief history of educational objectives. *Dialogos, 6,* 9–14.

Cartier-Bresson, H. (1952). *The decisive moment.* New York: Simon & Schuster.

Case, D. O. (2007). *Looking for information* (2nd ed.). Bingley, UK: Emerald.

Chambers, A. (2004). *Postcards from no man's land.* New York, NY: Speak.

Christenbury, L. (1990). No ivory towers: An open letter to Karen Jost. *English Journal, 79*(5), 30–31.

Christensen, L. (2000). *Reading, writing, and rising up: Teaching about social justice and the power of the written word.* Portland, OR: Rethinking Schools.

Christensen, L. (2009). *Teaching for joy and justice.* Portland, OR: Rethinking Schools.

Clinton, K., Jenkins, H., & McWilliams, J. (2013). New literacies in an age of participatory culture. In H. Jenkins & W. Kelley (Eds.), *Reading in a participatory culture* (pp. 3–23). New York: Teachers College Press.

Cochran-Smith, M., & Lytle, S. L. (1992). *Inside/outside: Teacher researcher and knowledge.* New York, NY: Teachers College Press.

Cochran-Smith, M., & Lytle, S. L. (2009). *Inquiry as stance: Practitioner research in the next generation.* New York, NY: Teachers College Press.

Collins, S. (2008). *The hunger games.* New York, NY: Scholastic.

Csikszentmihalyi, M. (2008). *Flow: The psychology of optimal experience.* New York, NY: HarperPerennial.

Cuban, L. (1986). *Teachers and machines: The classroom use of technology since 1920.* New York, NY: Teachers College Press.

Currey, M. (2013). *Daily rituals: How artists work.* New York, NY: Knopf.

Delpit, L. D. (1988). The silenced dialogue: Power and pedagogy in educating other people's children. *Harvard Educational Review, 58*(3), 280–298.

Delpit, L. (2006). *Other people's children: Cultural conflict in the classroom*. New York, NY: The New Press.

Delpit, L. (2013). *"Multiplication is for white people": Raising expectations for other people's children*. New York, NY: The New Press.

Dewey, J. (1897). The school and social process. In J. A. Boydston (Ed.), *The middle words: Essays on school and society, 1899–1901* (pp. 5–20). Carbondale, IL: Southern Illinois University Press.

Dewey, J. (1916). *Democracy and education: An introduction to the philosophy of education*. New York, NY: The Free Press.

Dewey, J. (1938). *Experience and education*. New York, NY: Simon and Schuster.

Dougherty, D. (n.d.). The maker mindset. Available at llk.media.mit.edu/courses/readings/maker-mindset.pdf

Everhart, R. B. (1983). *Reading, writing and resistance*. Boston, MA: Routledge.

Fecho, B. (2011). *Teaching for the students: Habits of heart, mind, and practice in the engaged classroom*. New York, NY: Teachers College Press.

Fecho, B., Collier, N. D., Friese, E., & Wilson, A. A. (2010). Critical conversations: Tensions and opportunities of the dialogical classroom. *English Education, 42*(4), 427–447.

Federal Communications Commission. (2010). The national broadband plan. Available at www.fcc.gov/national-broadband-plan

Feistritzer, C. E. (2011). *Profile of teachers in the U.S. 2011*. Washington, DC: National Center for Educational Information.

Filipiak, D. (2014). Shared purpose. In A. Garcia (Ed.), *Teaching in the connected learning classroom* (pp. 87–102). Irvine, CA: Digital Media and Learning Research Hub.

Fine, M. (2002). Civic lessons. UC Los Angeles: UCLA's Institute for Democracy, Education, and Access. Available at escholarship.org/uc/item/2ct0p7rw

Finn, P. J. (2009). *Literacy with an attitude: Educating working-class children in their own self-interest* (2nd ed.). New York, NY: State University of New York Press.

Fletcher, D. (2009). Brief history of standardized testing. *Time*. Available at content.time.com/time/nation/article/0,8599,1947019,00.html

Fordham, A., & Ogbu, J. U. (1986). Black students' school success: Coping with the "burden of acting White." *The Urban Review, 18*, 176–206.

Foucault, M. (1975). *Discipline and punish: The birth of the prison*. New York, NY: Vintage.

Freebody, P., & Luke, A. (1990). Literacies programs: Debates and demands in cultural context. *Prospect: Australian Journal of TESOL, 5*(7), 7–16.

Freebody, P., & Luke, A. (2003). Literacy as engaging with new forms of life: The "four roles" model. In G. Bull & M. Anstey (Eds.), *The literacy lexicon* (2nd ed., pp. 51–66). Frenchs Forest, NSW, Australia: Pearson Education.

Freire, P. (1970). *Pedagogy of the oppressed*. New York, NY: Herder and Herder.

Freire P. (1994). *Pedagogy of hope: Reliving pedagogy of the oppressed*. New York, NY: Continuum.

Freire, P. (2004). *Pedagogy of indignation*. London, UK: Paradigm Publishers.

Freire, P., & Macedo, D. (1987). *Literacy: Reading the word and the world*. Westport, CT: Bergin and Garvey.

Friedman, T. (2007). *The world is flat: A brief history of the twenty-first century*. New York: Farrar, Straus, & Giroux.

Gallagher, K. (2009). *Readicide: How schools are killing reading and what you can do about it.* Portland, ME: Stenhouse.

Garcia, A. (2012). Good reception: Utilizing mobile media and games to develop critical inner-city agents of social change. Unpublished doctoral dissertation, University of California, Los Angeles.

Garcia, A. (2013). *Critical foundations in young adult literature: Challenging genres.* Rotterdam, The Netherlands: Sense Publishers.

Garcia, A. (2014a). Academically oriented teaching. In A. Garcia (Ed.), *Teaching in the connected learning classroom* (pp. 39–54). Irvine, CA: Digital Media and Learning Research Hub.

Garcia, A. (Ed.). (2014b). *Teaching in the connected learning classroom.* Irvine, CA: Digital Media and Learning Research Hub.

Garcia, A., & O'Donnell-Allen, C. (2014). The Saving Our Stories project: Pushing beyond the culturally-neutral digital literacies of the Common Core. In J. Purdy & R. McClure (Eds.), *Next digital scholar: A fresh approach to the Common Core Standards in research and writing* (pp. 325–351). Medford, NJ: Information Today.

Gardner, H. (2011). *Creating minds: An anatomy of creativity seen through the lives of Freud, Einstein, Picasso, Stravinsky, Eliot, Graham, and Ghandi.* New York, NY: Basic.

Gartner, J. (2011). It all came down to this: "Know thyself, understand others" A first year teacher's journey through a new world. In P. R. Schmidt & A. M. Lazar (Eds.), *Practicing what we teach: How culturally responsive literacy classrooms make a difference* (pp. 56–68). New York, NY: Teachers College Press.

Gay, G. (2010). *Culturally responsive teaching: Theory, research, and practice.* New York, NY: Teachers College Press.

Gee, J. P. (2012). *Social linguistics and literacies: Ideology in discourses* (4th ed.). New York, NY: Routledge.

Ginwright, S. A. (2009). *Black youth rising: Activism and radical healing in urban America.* New York, NY: Teachers College Press.

Giroux, H. (2012). The war against teachers as public intellectuals in dark times. *Truthout.* Available at truth-out.org/opinion/item/13367-the-corporate-war-against-teachers-as-public-intellectuals-in-dark-times

Gladwell, M. (2010). Small change: Why the revolution will not be tweeted. *The New Yorker.* Available at newyorker.com/reporting/2010/10/04/101004fa_fact_gladwell?currentPage=all

Goffman, E. (1959). *The presentation of self in everyday life.* London, UK: Penguin Books.

Golden, J. (2001). *Reading in the dark: Using film as a tool in the English classroom.* Urbana, IL: National Council of Teachers of English.

Goldsmith, K. (2011). *Uncreative writing.* New York, NY: Columbia University Press.

Goldstein, D. (2014). *The teacher wars.* New York, NY: Doubleday.

Green, J. (2012). *The fault in our stars.* New York, NY: Speak.

Haddon, M. (2004). *The curious incident of the dog in the night-time.* New York, NY: Vintage.

Hamilton, B. J. (2013). Libraries as "sponsors of literacies": Diving deep to expose narratives & metanarratives. *DMLCentral.* Available at dmlcentral.net/blog/buffy-hamilton/libraries-%E2%80%98sponsors-literacies%E2%80%99-diving-deep-expose-narratives-metanarratives

Herrington, A., Hodgson, K., & Moran, C. (Eds.). (2009). *Teaching the new writing: Technology, change, and assessment in the 21st-century classroom.* New York, NY: Teachers College Press.

Hillenbrand, L. (2010). *Unbroken: A World War II story of survival, resilience, and redemption.* New York, NY: Random House.

Hillocks, G. (1995). *Teaching writing as reflective practice.* New York, NY: Teachers College Press.

hooks, b. (1994). *Teaching to transgress.* New York, NY: Routledge.

Hunt, B. (2012). Centering on essential lenses. *Bud the Teacher.* Available at budtheteacher.com/blog/2012/05/24/centering-on-essential-lenses/

Hunt, B. (2014). Openly networked. In A. Garcia (Ed.), *Teaching in the connected learning classroom* (pp. 71–86). Irvine, CA: Digital Media and Learning Research Hub.

Hutchinson, A. (2013). "Connecting, Curating and Changing" by high school English teacher Ashley Hutchinson from the Tar River Writing Project. Available at digitalis.nwp.org/resource/5227

Hymes, D. (1972). *Models of the interaction of language and social life.* In J. Gumperz & D. Hymes (Eds.), *Directions in sociolinguistics: The ethnography of communication* (pp. 35–71). New York: Holt, Rhinehart & Winston.

Ito, M., Matsuda, M., & Okabe, D. (Eds.). (2006). *Personal, portable, pedestrian: Mobile phones in Japanese life.* Cambridge, MA: MIT Press.

Ito, M., Gutiérrez, K., Livingstone, S., Penuel, B., Rhodes, J., Salen, K., . . . Watkins, S. C. (2013). *Connected learning: An agenda for research and design.* Irvine, CA: Digital Media and Learning Research Hub.

Jenkins, H. (1992). *Textual poachers: Television fans and participatory culture.* New York, NY: Routledge.

Jenkins, H. (2006). *The wow climax: Tracing the emotional impact of popular culture.* New York, NY: New York University Press.

Jenkins, H. (2008). *Convergence culture: Where old and new media collide.* New York, NY: New York University Press.

Jenkins, H., Clinton, K., Purushotma, R., Robison, A. J., & Weigel, M. (2009). *Confronting the challenges of participatory culture: Media education for the 21st century.* Chicago, IL: MacArthur Foundation.

Jenkins, H., Ford, S., & Green, J. (2013). *Spreadable media: Creating value and meaning in a networked culture.* New York, NY: New York University Press.

Jenkins, H., & Kelley, W. (2013). *Reading in a participatory culture: Remixing Moby Dick in the English classroom.* New York, NY: Teachers College Press.

Jocson, K. (2014). Critical media ethnography: Youth media research. In D. Paris & M. T. Winn (Eds.), *Humanizing research: Decolonizing qualitative inquiry with youth and communities* (pp. 105–123). Thousand Oaks, CA: SAGE Publications.

Joffe-Walt, C. (Producer). (2015, March 13). Three miles [radio broadcast episode]. *This American Life.* Available at thisamericanlife.org/radio-archives/episode/550/three-miles

Johnson, A. (2001). *Privilege, power, and difference.* Mountain View, CA: Mayfield.

Johnson, F. (2015). Common Core: A huge hurdle to education deal. Available at nationaljournal.com/congress/common-core-a-huge-hurdle-to-education-deal -20150128

John-Steiner, V. (1997). *Notebooks of the mind: Explorations of thinking.* New York, NY: Oxford University Press.

John-Steiner, V. (2006). *Creative collaboration.* Oxford, UK: Oxford University

Johnston, M. (2014). Transgender teen Leelah Alcorn: "My death needs to mean something." *The Boston Globe.* Available at bostonglobe.com/lifestyle /2014/12/31/transgender-teen-leelah-alcorn-death-needs-mean-something/ 4hw6uPd8NtjIbn8kAdyAbM/story.html

Jost, K. (1990). Why English teachers should not write. *English Journal, 79*(3), 65–66.

Kahne, J., Lee, N., & Feezell, J. T. (2012). Digital media literacy education and online civic and political participation. *International Journal of Communications, 6,* 1–24.

Kahne, J., Middaugh, E., & Evans, C. (2008). *The civic potential of video games.* Cambridge, MA: MIT Press.

Kajder, S. (2010). *Adolescents and digital literacies: Learning alongside our students.* Urbana, IL: National Council of Teachers of English.

King, Jr., M. L. (1963). Letter from a Birmingham jail. Available at africa.upenn.edu/ Articles_Gen/Letter_Birmingham.html

Kinloch, V. (2010). *Harlem on our minds: Place, race, and the literacies of urban youth.* New York, NY: Teachers College Press.

Kirkland, D. (2010). English(es) in urban contexts: Politics, pluralism, and possibilities. *English Education, 42*(3), 293–306.

Kligler-Vilenchik, N. (2013). "Decreasing world suck": Fan communities, mechanisms of translation, and participatory politics. Annenberg School for Communication and Journalism, University of Southern California. Available at dmlhub.net/publications/decreasing-world-suck-fan-communities-mechanisms -translation-and-participatory-politics/

Knaus, C. (2011). *Shut up and listen: Teaching writing that counts in urban schools.* New York, NY: Peter Lang.

Kozol, J. (2013). *Fire in the ashes: Twenty-five years among the poorest children in America.* New York, NY: Broadway Books.

Krest, M. (1990, September). The reflective writing teacher and the application of knowledge. *English Journal, 79*(5), 18–24.

Kuhlthau, C. C. (1993). *Seeking meaning: A process approach to library and information services.* Norwood, NJ: Ablex Publishing Corporation.

Lamott, A. (1995). *Bird by bird: Some instructions on writing and life.* New York, NY: Anchor Books.

Lankshear, C., & Knobel, M. (2004, April). *Text-related roles of the digitally "at home."* Paper presented at the annual meeting of the American Education Research Association, San Diego. Available at everydayliteracies.net/files/roles.html

Lave, J., & Wenger, E. (1991). *Situated learning: Legitimate peripheral participation.* Cambridge, UK: Cambridge University Press.

Leander, K. M. (2004). Reading the spatial histories of positioning in a classroom literacy event. In K. M. Leander & M. Sheehy (Eds.), *Spatializing literacy research and practice* (pp. 115–141). New York, NY: Peter Lang.

Leander, K. M. (2007). "You won't be needing your laptops today": Wired bodies in the wireless classroom. In M. Knobel & C. Lankshear (Eds.), *A new literacies sampler* (pp. 25–48). New York, NY: Peter Lang.

Lee, C. D. (1993). *Signifying as a scaffold for literary interpretation: The pedagogical implications of an African American discourse genre.* Urbana, IL: National Council of Teachers of English.

Lee, C. (2014). Production-centered classrooms. In A. Garcia (Ed.), *Teaching in the connected learning classroom* (pp. 55–70). Irvine, CA: Digital Media and Learning Research Hub.

Lee, S. (1989). Public Enemy's *Fight the Power.* Universal.

Lewin, K. (1943). Forces behind food habits and methods of change. *Bulletin of the National Research Council, 108,* 35–65.

Linton, A. L. (2015). Politically engaged and alienated youth: Reevaluating 2010 UK student protests. In B. Kirshner & E. Middaugh (Eds.), *#youthaction: Becoming political in the digital age* (pp. 191–207). Charlotte, NC: Information Age Publishing.

Lorde, A. (1984). The master's tools will never dismantle the master's house. In *Sister outsider: Essays & speeches by Audre Lorde* (pp. 110–113). Berkeley, CA: Crossing Press.

Luke, A., & Freebody, P. (2003). Literacy as engaging with new forms of life: The "four roles" model. In G. Bull & M. Anstey (Eds.), *The literacy lexicon* (2nd ed., pp. 51–66). Frenchs Forest, NSW, Australia: Pearson Education.

Mali, T. (2006). Taylor Mali on "What Teachers Make." Available at youtube.com/watch?v=RxsOVK4syxU.

Massey, D. S. (2008). *Categorically unequal: The American stratification system.* New York, NY: Russell Sage Foundation.

McIntosh, P. (2005). White privilege: Unpacking the invisible knapsack. In P. Rothenberg (Ed.), *White privilege: Essential readings on the other side of racism* (2nd ed., pp. 109–114). New York, NY: Worth.

McLuhan, M. (2011). *The Gutenberg galaxy.* Toronto: University of Toronto. (Original work published in 1962)

Meier, D. (2003). *In schools we trust: Creating communities of learning in an era of testing and standardization.* Boston, MA: Beacon Press.

Middaugh, E., Conner, J., Donahue, D., Harcia, A., Kahne, J., Kirshner, B., & Levine, P. (2012). Service & activism in the digital age: Supporting youth engagement in public life. *DML Central Working Papers.* Available at civicsurvey.org

Miller, A. (1953). *The crucible: A play in four acts.* New York, NY: Viking Press.

Miller, D. (2009). *The book whisperer: Awakening the inner reader in every child.* San Francisco, CA: Jossey-Bass.

Mirra, N. (2014). Interest-driven learning: Student identities and passions as gateways to connected learning. In A. Garcia (Ed.), *Teaching in the connected learning classroom* (pp. 10–24). Irvine, CA: Digital Media and Learning Research Hub.

Moje, E. B. (2004). Powerful spaces: Tracing the out-of-school literacy spaces of Latino/a youth. In K. M. Leander & M. Sheehy (Eds.), *Spatializing literacy research and practice* (pp. 15–38). New York, NY: Peter Lang.

Morozov, E. (2011). *Net delusion: The dark side of internet freedom.* New York, NY: PublicAffairs.

Morrell, E. (2004). *Linking literacy and popular culture: Finding connections for lifelong learning.* Norwood, MA: Christopher-Gordon Publishers.

Morrell, E. (2015). The 2014 NCTE presidential address: Powerful English at NCTE yesterday, today, and tomorrow: Toward the next movement. Available at ncte.org/library/NCTEFiles/Resources/Journals/RTE/0493-feb2015/RTE0493 Address.pdf

Morville, P. (2005). *Ambient findability: What we find changes who we become.* Sebastopol, CA: O'Reilly Media.

Myracle, L. (2011). *Shine.* New York, NY: Amulet.

National Commission on Excellence in Education. (1983). *A nation at risk: The imperative for educational reform.* Washington, DC: U.S. Government Printing Office.

National Commission on Writing. (2003). *The neglected "R": The need for a writing revolution.* New York, NY: College Entrance Examination Board.

National Council of Teachers of English. (1999). NCTE position statement on reading. Available at ncte.org/positions/statements/positiononreading

National Council of Teachers of English. (2005). NCTE position statement on multimodal literacies. Available at ncte.org/positions/statements/multimodalliteracies

National Council of Teachers of English. (2013). NCTE position statement on 21st-century literacies. Available at ncte.org/positions/statements/21stcentdefinition

National Council of Teachers of English. (n.d.). Teachers as readers: Forming book groups as professionals. Available at ncte.org/positions/statements/teachersasreaders

National Governors Association Center for Best Practices (NGACBP) & Council of Chief State School Officers (CCSSO). (2010). Common Core State Standards. Washington, DC: Authors.

National Writing Project. (2006). *Writing for a change: Boosting literacy and learning through social action.* San Francisco, CA: John Wiley & Sons, Inc.

New London Group. (1996). A pedagogy of multiliteracies: Designing social futures. *Harvard Educational Review, 66*(1), 60–92.

New London Group. (2000). A pedagogy of multiliteracies designing social futures. In B. Cope & M. Kalantizis (Eds.), *Multiliteracies: Literacy learning and the design of social futures* (pp. 9–37). New York, NY: Routledge.

Oakes, J. (1986). Beyond tracking. *Educational Horizons, 65*(1), 32–35.

O'Donnell-Allen, C. (2006). *The book club companion: Fostering strategic readers in the secondary classroom.* Portsmouth, NH: Heinemann.

O'Donnell-Allen, C. (2007). Research that makes a difference. *English Journal, 97*(2), 89–90.

O'Donnell-Allen, C. (2011). *Tough talk, tough texts: Teaching English to change the world.* Portsmouth, NH: Heinemann.

O'Donnell-Allen, C. (2012). The best writing teachers are writers themselves. *The Atlantic.* Available at theatlantic.com/national/archive/2012/09/the-best-writing-teachers-are-writers-themselves/262858/

O'Donnell-Allen, C. (2014). Peer supported learning. In A. Garcia (Ed.), *Teaching in the connected learning classroom* (pp. 25–38). Irvine, CA: Digital Media and Learning Research Hub.

Office of Language, Culture, and Equity. (2011). Culturally and linguistically diverse students in Colorado: A state of the state report. Available at www.cde.state.co.us/sites/default/files/documents/cdesped/download/pdf/cld_stateofthestate2011.pdf

Ogbu, J. (1991). Minority coping responses and school experience. *Journal of Psychohistory, 18*(4), 433–456.

Orfield, M. (2002). *American metropolitics: The new suburban reality.* Washington, DC: Brookings Institution Press.

Padilha, J. (2002). *Bus 174.* New York, NY: Virgil Films.

Paris, D. (2012). Culturally sustaining pedagogy: A needed change in stance, terminology, and practice. *Educational Researcher, 41*(3), 93–97.

Paris, D., & Alim, H. S. (2014). What are we seeking to sustain through culturally sustaining pedagogy?: A loving critique forward. *Harvard Educational Review, 84*(1), 85–100.

Paton, A. (1951). *Cry, the beloved country.* New York, NY: Scribner.

Paul, J. (2014). Jeffco students protest proposed "censorship" of history curriculum. *Denver Post.* Available at denverpost.com/news/ci_26582843/jeffco-students-skip-classes-protest-censorship-history-curriculum

Pendleton, C. S. (1924). *The social objectives of school English.* Nashville, TN: Self-published. Available at babel.hathitrust.org/cgi/pt?id=wu.89097627475;view=1up;seq=6

Peterson, R. E. (1991). Teaching how to read the world and change it: Critical pedagogy in the intermediate grades. In C. E. Walsh (Ed.), *Literacy as praxis: Culture, language, and pedagogy* (pp. 156–182). Norwood, NJ: Ablex Publishing.

Pfister, R. C. (2014). *Hats for house elves: Connected learning and civic engagement in Hogwarts at Ravelry.* Irvine, CA: Digital Media and Learning Research Hub.

Philip, T. M., & Garcia, A. (2013). The importance of still teaching the iGeneration: New technologies and the centrality of pedagogy. *Harvard Educational Review, 83*(2), 300–319.

Philip, T. M., & Garcia, A. (2014). Schooling mobile phones: Assumptions about proximal benefits, the challenges of shifting meanings, and the politics of teaching. *Educational Policy, 29*(4), 676–707.

Phillips, S. A. (1999). *Wallbangin': Graffiti and gangs in L.A.* Chicago, IL: University of Chicago Press.

Postman, N., & Weingartner, C. (1971). *Teaching as a subversive activity.* New York, NY: Dell Publishing.

Rami, M. (2014). *Thrive: 5 ways to (re)invigorate your teaching.* Portsmouth, NH: Heinemann.

Ravitch, D. (2010). *The death and life of the great American school system: How testing and choice are undermining education.* New York, NY: Basic Books.

Riley, E., Mehta, R., & Jenkins, H. (2013). *Flows of reading: Engaging with texts.* Available at scalar.usc.edu/anvc/flowsofreading/index

Romero, A., Cammarota, J., Dominguez, K., Valdez, L., Ramirez, G., & Hernandez, L. (2008). "The opportunity if not the right to see": The social justice education project. In J. Cammarota & M. Fine (Eds.), *Revolutionizing education: Youth participatory action research in motion* (pp. 131–150). New York, NY: Routledge.

Rong, X. L., & Preissle, J. (2009). *Educating immigrant students in the 21st century: What educators need to know* (2nd ed.). Thousand Oaks, CA: Corwin.

Rose, M. (1996). *Possible lives: The promise of public education in America.* New York, NY: Penguin Books.

Rose, M. (2009). *Why school? Reclaiming education for all of us.* New York, NY: The New Press.

Ruitenberg, C. (2009). Educating political adversaries: Chantal Mouffe and radical democratic citizenship education. *Studies in Philosophy and Education, 28*(3), 269–281.

Sanchez-Tranquilino, M. (1995). Space, power, and youth culture: Mexican American graffiti and Chicano murals in East Los Angeles, 1972–1978. In B. J. Bright & L. Bakewell (Eds.), *Looking high and low: Art and cultural identity* (pp. 55–88). Tucson, AZ: University of Arizona Press.

Sawyer, R. K. (2012). *Explaining creativity: The science of human innovation.* Oxford, UK: Oxford University Press.

Schneider, J. (2014). *From the ivory tower to the schoolhouse: How scholarship becomes common knowledge in education.* Boston, MA: Harvard University Press.

Schultz, K., Hodgin, E., & Paraiso, J. (2015). Blogging as civic engagement: Developing a sense of authority and audience in an urban public school classroom. In B. Kirshner & E. Middaugh (Eds.), *#youthaction: Becoming political in the digital age.* (pp. 147–168). Charlotte, NC: Information Age Publishing.

Serafini, F. (2012). Expanding the four resources model: Reading visual and multi-modal texts. *Pedagogies: An International Journal, 7*(2), 150–164.

Shakespeare, W. (2003). *Macbeth.* New York, NY: Simon & Schuster.

Shakespeare, W. (2004a). *Othello.* New York, NY: Simon & Schuster.

Shakespeare, W. (2004b). *Romeo and Juliet.* New York, NY: Simon & Schuster.

Shin, H. B., & Kominski, R. A. (2010). *Language use in the United States: 2007 American Community Survey Reports, ACS-12.* Washington, DC: U.S. Census Bureau.

Shor, I. (1987). *Critical teaching and everyday life.* Chicago, IL: University of Chicago Press.

Shor, I. (1993). Paulo Freire's political pedagogy. In P. Leonard & P. McLaren (Eds.), *Paulo Freire: A critical encounter* (pp. 24–35). New York, NY: Routledge.

Shor, I., & Freire, P. (1987). *A pedagogy for liberation.* Westport, CT: Bergin & Garvey.

Singer, J. (2006). *Stirring up justice: Writing and reading to change the world.* Portsmouth, NH: Heinemann

Skinner, B. F. (1961). Why we need teaching machines. *Harvard Educational Review, 31*(4), 377–398.

Smagorinsky, P. (2007). *Teaching English by design: How to create and carry out instructional units.* Portsmouth, NH: Heinemann.

Smagorinsky, P. (2009). Is it time to abandon the idea of "best practices" in the teaching of English? *English Journal, 98*(6), 15–22.

Smith, A. D. (1994). *Twilight: Los Angeles, 1992.* New York, NY: Anchor Books.

Smith, L. T. (1999). *Decolonizing methodologies: Research and indigenous peoples.* London, UK: Zed Books.

Stallworth, J., & Gibbons, L. C. (2012). What's on the list . . . now? A survey of book-length works taught in secondary schools. *English Leadership Quarterly, 34*(3), 2–3.

Stovall, D. (2006). From hunger strike to high school: Youth development, social justice, and school formation. In S. Ginwright, P. Noguera, & J. Cammarota (Eds.), *Beyond resistance! Youth activism and community change* (pp. 97–110). New York, NY: Routledge.

Tatum, A. W. (2006). Engaging African American males in reading. *Educational Leadership, 63*(5), 44–49.

Tatum, A. W. (2008). Discussing texts with adolescents in culturally responsive ways. In K. Hinchman & H. Sheridan-Thomas (Eds.), *Best practices in adolescent literacy instruction* (pp. 3–19). New York, NY: Guilford Press.

Tatum, A. W. (2009). *Reading for their life: (Re)building the textual lineages of African American adolescent males.* Portsmouth, NH: Heinemann.

Thein, A. H., Beach, R., & Parks, D. (2007). Perspective-taking as transformative practice in teaching multicultural literature to white students. *English Journal, 97*(2), 54–60.

Townes, C., & Petrohilos, D. (2014). Who police killed in 2014. *Think Progress.* Available at thinkprogress.org/justice/2014/12/12/3601771/people-police-killed-in-2014/

Turnbull, H. W. (Ed.). (2008). *The correspondence of Isaac Newton.* Cambridge, UK: Cambridge University Press.

UserExperienceWorks. (2011, Oct. 6). *A magazine is an iPad that does not work* [Video file]. Available at youtube.com/watch?v=aXV-yaFmQNk

Valdez, L. (1992). *Zoot suit and other plays.* Houston, TX: Arte Publico Press.

Van Lier, L. (2004). *The ecology and semiotics of language learning: A sociocultural perspective.* Boston, MA: Kluwer Academic Publishers.

Vygotsky, L. (1986). *Thought and language.* Boston, MA: MIT Press.

Walker, M. (1989). For my people. *This is my century: New and collected poems* (pp. 6–7). Athens, GA: University of Georgia Press.

Wark, M. (2004). *A hacker manifesto.* Boston, MA: Presidents of Harvard College.

Watkins, S. C. (2009). *The young and the digital: What the migration to social network sites, games, and anytime, anywhere media means for our future.* Cambridge, MA: MIT Press.

Wessling, S. B. (2011). *Supporting students in a time of Core Standards: Grades 9–12.* Urbana, IL: National Council of Teachers of English.

Westheimer, J. (2015). *What kind of citizen? Educating our children for the common good.* New York, NY: Teachers College Press.

Westheimer, J., & Kahne, J. (2004). What kind of citizen? The politics of educating for democracy. *American Educational Research Journal, 41*(2), 237–269.

White, G. (2007). *Yoga beyond belief: Insights to awaken and deepen your practice.* Berkeley, CA: North Atlantic Books.

Willis, P. (1981). *Learning to labor.* New York, NY: Columbia University Press.

Wingfield, N. (2014). Feminist critics of video games facing threats in "Gamer-Gate" campaign. *The New York Times.* Available at nytimes.com/2014/10/16/technology/gamergate-women-video-game-threats-anita-sarkeesian.html

Yancey, K. B. (2009). *Writing in the 21st century.* Urbana, IL: National Council of Teachers of English.

Zinn, H. (1994). *You can't be neutral on a moving train: A personal history of our times.* Boston, MA: Beacon Press.

Zusak, M. (2007). *The book thief.* New York, NY: Alfred A. Knopf.

Index

About the Authors

Antero Garcia is an assistant professor in the English department at Colorado State University. Prior to moving to Colorado, he was an English teacher at a public high school in South Central Los Angeles. Antero completed his Ph.D. in the Urban Schooling division of the Graduate School of Education and Information Studies at the University of California, Los Angeles. His research has appeared in numerous journals, including *The Harvard Educational Review*, *English Journal*, and *Teachers College Record*. He is the author of the book *Critical Foundations in Young Adult Literature: Challenging Genres* (2013) and editor of *Teaching in the Connected Learning Classroom* (2014).

Cindy O'Donnell-Allen is a full professor in the English department at Colorado State University, where she directs the CSU Writing Project. She was a secondary English teacher in Oklahoma for 11 years and became a member of the Oklahoma Writing Project in 1991. She is a National Writing Project Connected Learning Ambassador, has served on the National Writing Project Board of Directors, and formerly co-chaired the NWP Teacher Inquiry Communities Network. Cindy is the author of numerous articles, chapters, and two books—*Tough Talk, Tough Texts: Teaching English to Change the World* and *The Book Club Companion: Fostering Strategic Readers in the Secondary Classroom*—as well as a co-curator for *Teaching in the Connected Learning Classroom*.